Economics in America

OPPOSING VIEWPOINTS

OPPOSING VIEWPOINTS SERIES: Volume Twelve

David L. Bender
Gary E. McCuen, Editors

GREENHAVEN PRESS, INC.
1611 POLK ST. N.E.
MINNEAPOLIS, MINNESOTA 55413

99463   ISBN 0-912616-19-9 Paper Edition
ISBN 0-912616-38-5 Library Edition

TABLE OF CONTENTS

TABLE OF EXERCISES

A major emphasis of this book is on critical thinking skills. Discussion exercises included after readings are not laborious writing assignments. They are included to stimulate class discussion and individual critical thinking.

INTRODUCTION

The purpose of this book, and the **Opposing Viewpoints Series** as a whole, is to present the reader with alternative points of view on complex and sensitive issues.

Perhaps the best way to inform oneself is to analyze the positions of those who are regarded as experts and well studied on the issues. Every reader will approach this book with some opinions of his own on the issues debated within it. However, the educated and well informed person should be able to recognize not only his arguments but those with whom he disagrees, for if one does not completely understand his opponent's point of view he really does not fully understand his own.

A pitfall to avoid in considering alternative points of view is to regard one's own point of view as being merely common sense and the most rational stance, and the point of view of others as being only opinion and naturally wrong. It may be that their opinion is correct and that yours is in error.

Another pitfall to avoid in seeking the best solution when considering controversial issues, is that of closing your mind to the opinions of those whose views differ from yours. The best way to approach a dialogue is to make your primary purpose that of understanding the mind and arguments of the other person and not that of enlightening him with your solutions and convincing him of their correctness.

It is the editors' hope that the reader of this book will enjoy a deeper understanding of the issues debated and will appreciate the complexity of even seemingly simple issues when good and honest men disagree. This awareness is particularly important in a democratic society such as ours, where men enter into public debate to determine the common good. People with whom you disagree should not be regarded as enemies, but rather as friends who suggest a different path to a common goal.

We would also like to caution the reader about being unwilling to take a stand on an issue because of a lack of information. That is an excuse and not a reason. One never has enough information. However, one should always be ready to form an opinion from the facts at hand. One should also remain flexible and be able to alter his opinion when new facts indicate that this is necessary.

CHAPTER

MORALITY AND VALUES

THE BUSINESSMAN'S MORAL FAILURE

Louis Finkelstein

Dr. Finkelstein was Chancellor of the Jewish Theological Seminary of America from 1951 to 1972. He is presently Director of the Institute for Religious and Social Studies and President of the Conference of Science, Philosophy and Religion. He is the author of numerous scholarly works on Judaism.

Consider the following questions while reading:

1. According to the author, what are the moral sources of American economic strength?
2. What specific examples of moral decay does he claim exists?
3. How does he suggest businessmen might improve their moral insights and behavior?

Louis Finkelstein, "The Businessman's Moral Failure," **Fortune**, September, 1958, p. 116. Reprinted with permission.

If American businessmen are right in the way most of them now live, then all the wise men of the ages, all the prophets and the saints were fools. If the saints were not fools, the businessmen must be.

Too many businessmen never stop to ponder what they are doing; they reject the need for self-discipline; they are satisfied to be clever, when they need to be wise. They worry about their place on the economic ladder, but are not concerned sufficiently with whether the civilization in which they work is likely to collapse. They can defeat a local competitor, but may well be defeated by the competitor of us all, which is moral decay.

Now the American executive is very often a man of some vision, motivated by a spirit that generates great energy. Underlying the efficiency of our business community there is the principle of teamwork, cooperation, a reasonable degree of pleasure in the success of co-workers, a comparatively broad welcome to talent, and freedom in human relationships. Granted, these are virtues of no mean order. But the American businessman is losing his insight into the moral sources of American economic strength.

Our country could not have reached its present heights without the blessing of natural resources; but the U.S. would have failed at the outset without a philosophy developed by men more concerned with the betterment of the human spirit than the comforts of the body. These men were inspired by the writings of immortal philosophers and religious thinkers. The modern business leader is more often than not bewildered at the suggestion that the future of the Republic is in some way related to the ideals and ideas of John Locke, not to mention Spinoza, the medieval Scholastics, the Rabbinic sages, and the ancient Greek philosophers.

Ask the U.S. businessman why he is successful today, and he may explain to you the advantages of capitalism, the profit motive, and the "American system." He may, with due modesty, point out the superiority of his own products and marketing. But he will largely ignore the philosophy foundations of the American system. He tends to ignore the great ethical laws as they apply immediately to his work. The truth is that he is preoccupied chiefly with gain, coasting on the spiritual momentum of the past, divorced from our

5

Reprinted with permission from **The Daily World**.

sources of inspiration. He is the leading citizen of a largely hedonistic nation propelled by meaningless drives toward materialistic and frequently meaningless goals.

Clearly no institution will survive if it is dedicated *only* to self-preservation. A business has a goal beyond simple success. It is not a biological organism whose survival is a virtue in itself. Rather, it is a man-created institution, an integral part of our culture, and as such must make a contribution of service to society (as well as a profit for itself) if it hopes to survive. It cannot do this out of a focus on self-gain or pride.

Why do I single out the American businessman for indictment, when he is probably no more materialistic than any of the rest of us? I do so because of the responsibility he bears, because his role in American society is so great. Ours is an industrial society, and the customs and morals and attitudes of businessmen pervade our whole life. Virtually all of us in America have adopted in some degree the pragmatic ethical standards of our business society; and to that degree we have abandoned our ethical and religious traditions.

THE AMERICAN TRAGEDY

Our American tragedy is that we fail to see the signs of our decay. But the signs are apparent in the vulgar ostentation all around us,...

The most casual observer is aware of the transgressions that go on daily in the American business community. He hears of tax returns that are outright perjury; he hears of purchasing agents who are taking bribes from suppliers, of businessmen offering bribes for false testimony or for police protection of some dubious enterprise. He reads of industries attempting to suborn state legislators for favorable legislation. He reads of businessmen bestowing favors on government officials to win special privileges. Even in my ivory tower on Morningside Heights, I have been urged by businessmen to accept a gift for the Theological Seminary in return for admitting a student — and have been threatened by withdrawal of contributions to the school if I failed to do so.

We hear of businessmen using wire taps to obtain information about their competitors, of management acting in collusion with racketeers, of men using prostitution to promote the sale of their goods. We hear of businessmen violating the most elementary requirements of city building codes and profiting from rat-infested tenements. We hear of financiers deliberately lying about their operations and the financial condition of their companies to mislead investors so that insiders can make killings in stock.

There are less overt practices in the business community that may appear to be only on the borderline of unethical behavior: for example, concealing the true price of goods behind time-payment schemes that are

7

actually usurious; employing advertising that is actually a flagrant misrepresentation of a product's worth. These and other clever dodges are accepted by many as normal phases of competition.

MORAL LAWS, NOT ECONOMIC LAWS

This market system is far more productive and efficient than state-controlled economies — yet the fact is that it is no longer a free market, despite all the pretensions. The great industrial combines see to it that nothing the farmer buys ever comes down in price, just as supermarkets retreat but little when high prices are once fixed on meat, bread, milk, butter. Meanwhile in the middle the farmer and consumer are squeezed and played upon like an accordion.

Industries that manufacture fertilizer, tractors, autos, tires and the oil corporations, the food processors, syndicate bakeries and canneries, the steel, aluminum and paper makers — all these, with their interlocking directorships, are boosting prices now in anticipation of higher oil costs. And also the big banks are raising their prime rates. All admit to surpluses and, for nearly all, profits still abound. Meanwhile, the small businessman, the distributor, the farmer and the consumer must accept the pressure clamped on them while the strong protect themselves. It is our belief and that of an increasing number of eminent economist-philosophers that —

Economic laws give way here to moral law. Rampant greed has a way of devouring itself. Officials of scores of the largest corporations have been and are under indictment for bribery and other financial illegalities, some of them so big and so close to the Administration and Pentagon that they may prove immune to prosecution though they confess to millions spent to bribe foreign officials into buying U.S. war planes. Several large grain corporation executives and wholesale beef operators are under indictment for embezzlement and theft — such a list could be very long. Fortunately however there are other industrial leaders and Government officials, men of conscience, who are disturbed.... The world's most distinguished economists now believe that economics has become a study in ethics and morals. We believe this has become the most important development of our day.

Graduate schools of business in some 50 universities are planning special courses in business morality and ethics this coming year for the first time. And they are doing so at the urging of groups of industrial and financial leaders. A survey by the N.Y. Times of lawyers, business and religious figures indicates a real awakening with emphasis on the need for official action — both national and international to prevent the further disintegration of the ethical base of the capitalist system.

Charles A. Wells, **Between the Lines**, September 15, 1975.

I would not deny that competition is the basis of our free enterprise and of our industrial success. Competition surely induces better efforts and great production. But to compete in ways that are designed to destroy someone else is very different from competing in terms of doing better than your rival....

Each of us has only one life on earth. When that life is used unwisely, the loss is irreparable for oneself and for one's fellows.

A businessman who understands these truths will develop an almost automatic pattern of behavior. Certain ancient rules apply with equal force to Jew and Christian, atheist and agnostic, to all men in all situations. These immutable laws are expressed in various ways. The Pentateuch reveals the Decalogue and the Golden Rule of Leviticus 19:18: ''Thou shalt love thy neighbor as thyself,'' which the Gospels restate in Matthew 7:12: ''All things whatsoever ye would that

9

men should do to you, do ye even so to them.'' Similar commandments are promulgated in the literature of the other great traditions of East and West.

Yet these and other binding commandments are often violated in the American business community. A man fears he may be risking his business if he obeys them, forgetting, however, that if he violates them he risks the world....

The American businessman, then, should literally *place ethics on the agenda* — for himself at home and in the office, for his company and trade association:

His calendar should include regular meetings of management to discuss the moral dimensions in his specific business....

He should seek expert advice on ethics. Existing resources in the field will gladly be made available to him.

He should put moral health on the same level as mental and physical health, indeed above them. This means he should read literature dealing with ethics; devote time to the study of ethics, alone and with colleagues and scholars; work for the establishment of research in ethics, as he has worked magnificently for the development of research in science and technology.

READING

THE GOLDEN RULE IS NOT THE BEST GUIDE FOR BUSINESSMEN

Craig C. Lundberg

Professor Lundberg teaches in the School of Management of the School of Business at Oregon State University. He is on the editorial board of the Academy of Management Review and has authored over sixty articles that have appeared in business and sociological journals.

As you read try to answer the following questions:

1. How does the author define the Golden Rule?
2. What are the three major assumptions behind the Golden Rule?
3. According to the author, how should one apply the Golden Rule in business and human affairs?

Craig C. Lundberg, ''The Golden Rule and Business Management: Quo Vadis?'' **Economic and Business Bulletin**, January 1968, pp. 36-40. Reprinted with permission from the author and the **Journal of Economics and Business**. **The Economic and Business Bulletin** is now called **Journal of Economics and Business**.

As I have talked with business managers I have been impressed that the vast majority of these men propose the Golden Rule as the most important guide for organizational behavior. Certainly this maxim is well-known as a guide for human conduct, yet regardless of its popularity we might question its adequacy as a business policy. Let me focus this paper by contrasting two sets of reasoning:

> The Golden Rule is the best general prescription for regulating human relationships, therefore, it is a good maxim for behavior in business especially within complex modern organization settings. The Golden Rule is a guide for human relations which is very limited in its applications in modern society. It must be applied with caution or not at all in contemporary business practice.

In the pages to follow I will note how the reasoning supporting the first assertion is generally believed, but will rely on my frame of reference as a social scientist to argue in favor of the second position. To do this I will differentiate between the Golden Rule as a religious norm and as a guide to ethical fairness in exchange relationships....

RELIGIOUS UNIVERSALITY OF THE GOLDEN RULE

While familiar the Golden Rule is stated in numerous forms. The book of Matthew, for instance, states that: "All things whatsoever ye would that men should do to you, do ye so unto them: for this is the Law and the Prophets." The medieval Biblical injunction, "Love they neighbor as thyself" has of course been most commonly interpreted with the contemporary maxim, "Do unto others as you would like them to do unto you."

We should not assume that the Golden Rule is primarily associated with Christianity for most other religions carry some version of it. In the Talmud, for example, we find, "What is hateful to you, do not do to your fellow man. That this is the entire law; all the rest is commentary." Confucianism, too, in the Analects has, "Surely it is the maxim of loving kindness: do not unto others that you would not have them do unto you." Buddhism in the Udana-Yarga says, "Hurt not others in ways that you yourself would find hurtful." Islam joins the chorus with, ''Not one of you is a believer until he desires for his brother that which he desires for himself.'' And in the Mahabharata the Brahman injunction says, ''This is the sum of duty: do not do unto others which would cause you pain if done to you.'' And so we see that the Golden Rule exists throughout the major religions of mankind.

THE RULE AS A GUIDE FOR EXCHANGES

We must at this point distinguish between the Jewish-Christian norm of brotherly love and the Golden Rule of fairness-ethics.[1] The Biblical

''Love thy neighbor as thyself,''

is a norm of Jewish-Christian brotherly love; it means love your neighbor, that is, to feel responsible for and at one with him. The Golden Rule as interpreted today is quite different. Perhaps it is no accident that the Golden Rule has become one of the most popular religious maxims of today because it can be interpreted in terms of fairness-ethics, which sounds a great deal like the religious maxims, but which in fact has quite a different meaning, namely, be fair in your exchanges with others. Contrast with the religious norm is complete for fairness-ethics means do not feel responsible and at one, but feel distant and separate; respect the rights of your neighbor, but do not love him. This differentiation between religious norm and a maxim of fairness-ethics is made so that we can focus on the latter, which is the principle or generalization in the fields of human relations as conceived by business management today.

DISTORTIONS AND CHANGES IN MEANING

The Golden Rule is very well known in western culture; it is a fairness-ethics injunction and it is usually accepted unquestioning. Although probably the most revered of common sense generalizations handed down by our industrial forebears, Golden Rule has not gone unthought about or completely unchallenged. As our society has become more liberal and the value of individual work has been widened to include a value of

[1] This point has been nicely made by Erich Fromm in **The Art of Loving**, page 130.

13

individual differences, the Golden Rule has been revamped....

In a recent graduate course and in a recent executive development program for middle managers, I asked participants to write out the versions of the Golden Rule known to them. The response was overwhelming and reflects and shows how far the Golden Rule has pervaded the mainstream of our business culture, everything from "an eye for an eye, a tooth for a tooth" to "every girl has a father"; from "You pat my back, I'll pat yours but you pat me first" to "drive carefully, the life you save may be your own"; from "The only way to have a friend is to be one" to "owe no man anything." Variations are reported implicit in our everyday petitions for help, such as "Share the United way" or "Give blood, the gift of life"; and we find variations in advertising such as one card manufacturer who asks that you give his card to show you care enough to send the very best, and of course there are even business philosophies such as the Murray D. Lincoln's "Intelligent selfishness."...[2]

ON APPLYING THE GOLDEN RULE

We see that from a religious origin strained through the web and woof of an industrial society the Golden Rule has come to reside in humor, in philosophy, and common sense, in fact nearly all arenas of contemporary life. The question still remains, however, is it a useful imperative? Can we take it as a generalized principle of, or guide for, human relationships? Let us now examine a few simple situations which, while hypothetical, could very well exist, and as we look at them let us ask ourselves about the utility of applying the Golden Rule in each case.

Picture a janitor and the president of a major corporation approaching the lobby doors of the corporation's downtown headquarters building. The two men approach the doors simultaneously. Who will open the door for whom and with what effects on the men?

Consider the marketing vice president of a major American business firm promptly arriving at the

2 Murray D. Lincoln, **Vice President of Charge of Revolution**.

stated time for an appointment with an executive of potentially the largest purchaser of his product in Venezuela. After an hour and a half of waiting the v.p. actively considers leaving.

Consider the personnel manager of a local company picking up his telephone to hear his counterpart in a competitor's firm asking if he would provide a summer job for the other man's high school age son.

Picture a computer expert who is new to a business deciding not to include certain critical information in his first report to his superior because he thinks it might jeopardize the existence of his function in the firm.

In the hypothetical examples above the parties have represented different organizational statuses, different cultures, different personal needs and capabilities for action, and different constraints on their behavior. In each example a literal application of the Golden Rule would be rather difficult for most reasonable people — they would feel the pressures of expectations and no doubt worry about the consequences to their responses to these situations. Perhaps these examples force us to wonder as to the universal application of the rule, and perhaps to question the assumption on which it is based. Let us now turn to this latter aspect.

ASSUMPTION BEHIND THE GOLDEN RULE

One assumption in the Golden Rule is that the "others" in an exchange situation are in fact capable of reciprocating the behavior. We quickly remember that persons are not equal in terms of abilities, at least adults, and clearly are not equally capable in terms of the organizational power they command. You might go on with this assumption and ask whether the "others" are in fact motivated to reciprocate, that is, whether they would want to return similar behaviors if it were possible too. *A second assumption* would be that either party to an exchange really understands the consequences to the behavior — how, in fact, will the others really feel and think. This is of course contingent on their having similar goals or aims, and in most cases this seems extremely unlikely. *A third major assumption* is that the Golden Rule assumes that other rules are not being violated whether they be formal, explicit rules or other implicit perhaps informal ones, such as custom. Take the privilege and duty which come with certain statuses in our society, perhaps illustrated in the first example above. Today, too, we have a widespread understanding that business practice should not include reciprocity in regard to purchasing, for example, and this may in certain instances conflict with the Golden Rule injunction. *A fourth assumption* has to do with the assumed similarity of preference or taste of the parties to the Golden Rule. One could confuse or sadden, hurt, or disadvantage another who did not have somewhat similar preferences or tastes, that is, values and interests like ours. Cross cultural examples often make this point clearly....[3]

EVALUATION OF THE GOLDEN RULE

We have seen that the Golden Rule, at least as a maxim of fairness-ethics, is extremely popular, and widely applied in our industrial society. By means of some hypothetical illustrations and by examining more directly the assumption behind and the lack of clarity in the Golden Rule we have also been able to offer some comment on the adequacy of this rule as a general principle of organizational behavior. I believe that we have demonstrated that the Golden Rule cannot be taken as a categorical imperative, that in fact one would have to be extremely careful in applying it in business and other human affairs.

[3] See many interesting examples in E. T. Hall, **The Silent Language**, 1959.

SMALL IS BEAUTIFUL

E. F. Schumacher

E. F. Schumacher is an economist who has directed international attention to value considerations in economics. His book **Small Is Beautiful: Economics As If People Mattered**, originally published in England, has become a best seller since its 1975 publication in the U.S.

Think of the following questions while you read:

1. What theory of prosperity was the author brought up on?
2. What does he say are the virtues of smallness?
3. How does he describe today's idolatry?

E.F. Schumacher, **Small Is Beautiful: Economics as if People Mattered** (New York: Harper & Row, 1973), pp. 63-66, 74-75, 293. Copyright © 1973 by E.F. Schumacher. Reprinted by permission.

I was brought up on an interpretation of history which suggested that in the beginning was the family; then families got together and formed tribes; then a number of tribes formed a nation; then a number of nations formed a "Union" or "United States" of this or that; and that, finally, we could look forward to a single World Government....

Second, I was brought up on the theory that in order to be prosperous a country had to be big — the bigger the better....

And third, I was brought up on the theory of the "economies of scale" — that with industries and firms, just as with nations, there is an irresistible trend, dictated by modern technology, for units to become ever bigger. Now, it is quite true that today there are more large organizations and probably also bigger organizations than ever before in history; but the number of small units is also growing and certainly not declining in countries like Britain and the United States, and many of these small units are highly prosperous and provide society with most of the really fruitful new developments....

Even today, we are generally told that gigantic organizations are inescapably necessary; but when we look closely we can notice that as soon as great size has been created there is often a strenuous attempt to attain smallness within bigness. The great achievement of Mr. Sloan of General Motors was to structure this gigantic firm in such a manner that it became, in fact, a federation of fairly reasonably sized firms. In the British National Coal Board, one of the biggest firms of Western Europe, something very similar was attempted under the chairmanship of Lord Robens; strenuous efforts were made to evolve a structure which would maintain the unity of one big organization and at the same time create the "climate" or feeling of there being a federation of numerous "quasi-firms." The monolith was transformed into a well-coordinated assembly of lively, semi-autonomous units, each with its own drive and sense of achievement. While many theoreticians — who may not be too closely in touch with real life — are still engaging in the idolatry of large size, with practical people in the actual world there is a tremendous longing and striving to profit, if at all possible, from the convenience, humanity, and

18

manageability of smallness. This, also, is a tendency which anyone can easily observe for himself....

MATERIALISM

In the excitement over the unfolding of his scientific and technical powers, modern man has built a system of production that ravishes nature and a type of society that mutilates man. If only there were more and more wealth, everything else, it is thought, would fall into place. Money is considered to be all-powerful; if it could not actually buy non-material values, such as justice, harmony, beauty or even health, it could circumvent the need for them or compensate for their loss. The development of production and the acquisition of wealth have thus become the highest goals of the modern world in relation to which all other goals, no matter how much lip-service may still be paid to them, have come to take second place. The highest goals require no justification; all secondary goals have finally to justify themselves in terms of the service their attainment renders to the attainment of the highest.

This is the philosophy of materialism, and it is this philosophy — or metaphysic — which is now being challenged by events. There has never been a time, in any society in any part of the world, without its sages and teachers to challenge materialism and plead for a different order of priorities.

For his different purposes man needs many different structures, both small ones and large ones, some exclusive and some comprehensive. Yet people find it most difficult to keep two seemingly opposite necessities of truth in their minds at the same time. They always tend to clamour for a final solution, as if in actual life there could ever be a final solution other than death. For constructive work, the principal task is always the restoration of some kind of balance. Today, we suffer from an almost universal idolatry of giantism. It is therefore necessary to insist on the virtues of smallness — where this applies. (If there were a prevailing idolatry of smallness, irrespective of subject or purpose, one would have to try and exercise influence in the opposite direction....

The economics of giantism and automation is a leftover of nineteenth-century conditions and nineteenth-century thinking and it is totally incapable of solving any of the real problems of today. An entirely new system of thought is needed, a system based on attention to people, and not primarily attention to goods — (the goods will look after themselves!). It could be summed up in the phrase, "production by the masses, rather than mass production." What was impossible, however, in the nineteenth-century, is possible now. And what was in fact — if not necessarily at least understandably — neglected in the nineteenth-century is unbelievably urgent now. That is, the conscious utilization of our enormous technological and scientific potential for the fight against misery and human degradation — a fight in intimate contact with actual people, with individuals, families, small groups, rather than states and other anonymous abstractions. And this presupposes a political and organizational structure that can provide this intimacy.

What is the meaning of democracy, freedom, human dignity, standard of living, self-realization, fulfillment? Is it a matter of goods, or of people? Of course it is a matter of people. But people can be themselves only in small comprehensible groups. Therefore we must learn to think in terms of an articulated structure that can cope with a multiplicity of small-scale units. If economic thinking cannot grasp this it is useless. If it cannot get beyond its vast abstractions, the national income, the rate of growth, capital/output ratio, input-output analysis, labor mobility, capital accumulation; if it cannot get beyond all this and make contact with the human realities of poverty, frustration, alienation, despair, breakdown, crime, escapism, stress, congestion, ugliness, and spiritual death, then let us scrap economics and start afresh.

Are there not indeed enough "signs of the times" to indicate that a new start is needed?

READING

ECONOMIC GROWTH IS NECESSARY

Rudolf Klein

Rudolf Klein is a Senior Fellow at the Center for Studies in Social Policy in London, where he was previously an editor and writer for **The Observer**.

Bring the following questions to your reading:

1. Why does the author say an economic philosophy of nongrowth would promote social conflict?
2. What does he say about the relationship between zero population growth (ZPG) and zero economic growth (ZEG)?
3. According to the author, what are some of the risks of a zero economic growth society?

Rudolf Klein, ''The Trouble With a Zero-Growth World,'' **New York Times Magazine**, June 2, 1974, pp. 14 + . © 1974 by The New York Times Company. Reprinted by permission.

One of the dangers of swings in intellectual fashions is that ideas become accepted before their implications have begun to be explored, as yesterday's unconventional wisdom becomes transmuted into today's unquestioned orthodoxy. The success of the advocates of non-growth in bringing about a mass conversion to their view is a case in point....

While modern societies are beginning, if all too slowly and hesitantly, to learn how to cope with some of the consequences of growth (like dealing with pollution), they are utterly unprepared to deal with the effects of nongrowth. Yet these effects, particularly if they are unanticipated and undiscussed, could be shattering. It is not all that difficult to sketch out a scenario of social catastrophe in a nongrowth society to equal, in its horror, the scenario of ecological catastrophe in a growth society.

The starting point of such a doomsday scenario would be the Hobbesian assumption that politics in societies like the United States is about the allocation of resources. There are different groups — some ethnically defined, some economically defined — struggling to improve their position in society, as measured by their incomes, their housing, their access to education, job opportunities and so on. At present, economic growth tends to blunt the edge of this conflict. For everyone can expect to be better off next year than they were last year, even if their relative position does not change. Furthermore, it is possible for some groups actually to improve their relative position, without anyone actually being worse off in terms of hard cash. The competition for resources (social and financial) is therefore a game in which everyone can win at least something.

Now imagine the situation transformed by a decision to halt all economic growth. Immediately the competition for resources becomes a zero-sum game. One man's prize is another man's loss. If the blacks want to improve their share of desirable goods, it can only be at the expense of the whites. If the over-65's are to be given higher pensions, or improved medical services, it can only be at the expense of the working population or of the young.

From this, it would seem only too likely that the

haves would man the barricades to defend their share of resources, against the have-nots. The politics of compromise would be replaced by the politics of revolution, because the have-nots would be forced to challenge the whole basis of society, and its distribution of wealth and power. For those who think that this distribution is wrong — and that most of the compromises are cosmetic anyway — this would be a welcome confrontation; not so, however, for those who take a more optimistic view of the possibilities of change in the existing society.

But the tensions created by nongrowth within a single political society like the United States would be compounded, more catastrophically still, within the international political community. For again, economic growth creates at least the possibility — even if in practice it has turned out to be illusory for some nations — of a general and continuing rise in standards of living. To abjure growth, by freezing the present situation, is thus to repudiate hope. It is to condemn a majority of the globe's inhabitants to permanent poverty unless (once again) the have-nots successfully manage to challenge the haves in order to bring about a redistribution of global resources in their own favor....

Nongrowth is a deceptively simple slogan. It would seem to imply a combination of zero population growth (Z.P.G.) and zero economic growth (Z.E.G.) — by which is usually meant, no further rise in the total population nor in such conventional indicators as the Gross National Product. This, in turn, would seem to suggest a rather unthreatening picture of a society continuing to enjoy its present standards of living which, in the case of the United States at any rate, are luxuriously high for the great majority. But, forgetting for a moment the international setting and making a start with the case of a single society like the United States, this particular intellectual ball of wool turns out to be a remarkable tangle which requires teasing out.

The first difficulty comes in trying to relate the two components of the stable society — Z.P.G. and Z.E.G. — to each other. If it is assumed that progress towards these two aims will proceed harmoniously in step, then it follows that no one's standards of living (as measured by per capita income) will fall — and the stable society appears as a well-cushioned resting place, a plausible setting for the optimistic scenario. But it is at least possible that economic growth might stop before population growth; indeed more than likely, since it is impossible to insure a stable population in the absence of compulsory abortion or euthanasia. If so, there would actually be a fall in per capita income. In turn, this would raise some exceedingly awkward questions as to whose income should be cut: the pessimistic, social and political cutthroat scenario would seem to be rather opposite in such an event....

It is implausible to assume that the present economy will remain as a mummified museum piece for perpetuity, that the United States will forever go on churning out the same number of cars, television sets, Ph.D.'s and garage mechanics. A stable society does not mean a frozen society, one hopes. But allowing for the possibility — indeed necessity — of change, how is such change to be controlled? For stability does imply control. It predicates that if Firm X (or University Y) produces too much in the way of goods, then Firm Z (or University W) will have to cut production back, if the total is not to be exceeded. It means that, if health and public services are to expand and improve in quality, the resources will have to be found by cutting other items of consumption.

The last point underlines the fact that progress from a growth to a stable society is also likely to mean progress from a society in which most of the decisions are taken by individuals or individual firms to a society where most of the decisions are taken collectively. It means (if we are really serious about Z.E.G.) more central control over the production and allocation of resources....

At this stage in the argument, however, it is necessary to reveal yet another concealed assumption. So far, I have tended to accept what might be called the social-engineering view of social change: that, given the political will and a little tinkering with the machinery of administration, it is practically possible to bring about certain desired changes. Only the self-evident difficulties of persuading a population to accept the personal implications of the general idea of Z.P.G. have been touched on so far.

But, in returning to Z.E.G., it is far from clear that

in the present state of knowledge, it is actually possible to exercise the sort of precise, finger-tip control which is implied by the idea of non-growth. The evidence, rather, appears to point in the opposite direction. But if, in fact, the economy continues to perform on a cyclical pattern, then it would seem — if Z.E.G. is to retain any meaning at all — that if by some unfortunate mishap the economy were to grow in one year, there would have to be a compensating fall in the following year. The manic-depressive pattern of economic management of recent decades might well be reinforced, with deeper and sharper recessions deliberately engineered to compensate for accidental growth — what might be called an economic abortion program. In turn, such a policy of economic management would once more entail political friction, deepening rather than narrowing divisions between the various economic, ethnic and social groups in American society....

No-growth in the United States means less growth elsewhere, given the nature of the world economy. In effect, therefore, the United States would be taking a paternalistic decision with damaging effect on much poorer nations (again, it's worth noting that, just as expenditure on improving the environment shows up in the national accounts, so does expenditure on foreign aid — and that both might be a casualty of Z.E.G.). Leaving aside the morality of such a course, it obviously has considerable implications for American foreign policy and the balance of power throughout the world. Economic isolationism implies political isolationism.

Abandoning this particular scenario, therefore, and accepting that the United States is inescapably a member of the global community, it then follows that the problems of a nongrowth society have to be considered in this wider context. The sorts of difficulties which have been discussed within the setting of a single country must now be translated in terms applicable to international society. Again, there are the problems of distribution — this time not as between ethnic groups and social classes, but as between different countries. Again, there are the problems of enforcing policy decisions — this time not in terms of strengthening the governmental machine of a single country but the mechanisms of international control. It hardly needs pointing out that while all the problems would be that much more severe, the means for tackling them are at present effectively nonexistent.

Indeed, what does the concept of a stable society imply when applied to the world community? Obviously the idea of Z.P.G. has even more urgency when applied on a global scale than in the case of a single country like the United States, since it is the soaring numbers in the underdeveloped and developing countries which help to perpetuate their poverty. Equally obviously, though, the difficulties of actually enforcing such a policy are compounded; indeed it is seen by some countries, notably by China, as a threat to their power.

But it is the idea of Z.E.G. on a global scale which is politically implausible. This would in effect mean condemning the majority of the world's population to poverty for the rest of time. But if this is a nonsense way of interpreting global Z.E.G., who is to decide which nations get how much? Who will ration out permission for growth? What are the standards — in terms of per capita income — which are going to be the upper limit of permissible growth?...

Leaning on history, this scenario might then suggest that a society which had adopted the values of nongrowth would be introvert rather than extrovert, traditional rather than innovative. Whether it had settled for an egalitarian distribution of wealth or for the perpetuation of inequalities, it would be resistant to change, stressing social control as the inevitable counterpart of social stability. There would be little social mobility, since this tends to be a product of economic growth. There might well evolve a gerontocracy, with power going hand in hand with seniority, since it would no longer be open to the young to secede from existing organizations to start their own. The only frontiers that would be open for exploration would be those of artistic or spiritual activity.

The resemblance of the picture to medieval society in Western Europe is not accidental. For that was a society which was based on nongrowth, whose mold was indeed broken only when the Protestant ethic of economic achievement became the ideology of the newly developing capitalism. It would be absurd to push the parallel too far; a society which commands technological resources of infinite potential, but refrains from using them to their full limits to create extra economic wealth, cannot be equated with one which was ravaged by starvation and the plague. But perhaps it is worth remembering that building cathedrals can go hand in hand with burning heretics, that emphasizing spiritual rather than material values does not necessarily imply tolerance, that a sense of community may be achieved at the cost of accepting social hierarchy.

This is not to imply that nongrowth will, inevitably, bring about such a situation — any more than growth will, inevitably, bring about ecological disaster. It is to suggest, however, that nongrowth may carry certain social and political risks just as growth may carry certain ecological dangers, and that it may need a determined effort to avoid both.

WE NEED LAWS AGAINST CORPORATE BRIBES

William Proxmire

William Proxmire is a Democratic Senator from Wisconsin. He has been a prominent liberal spokesman in the Senate on economic and tax related issues.

Think of the following questions while you read:

1. What is the Foreign Payments Disclosure Act?
2. How does Senator Proxmire justify his support of this bill?
3. How do you interpret the cartoon in this reading?

Senator William Proxmire, **Congressional Record**, March 25, 1976.

Recently I introduced a bill, S. 3133, which I am calling "the Foreign Payments Disclosure Act." This proposed legislation requires business firms subject to the Securities Exchange Act to disclose any payment in excess of $1,000 paid to a foreign government official, a foreign political party or candidate for foreign political office, or to an agent hired to obtain business with a foreign government.

In addition, the Foreign Payments Disclosure Act makes it unlawful for a business firm to make a payment to a foreign government official for the purpose of obtaining business, or to make a payment to a foreign political party or candidate for the purpose of obtaining business from a foreign government.

In the near future the Committee on Banking, Housing and Urban Affairs will schedule hearings on this bill.

All of us are aware of the numerous disclosures and revelations of foreign bribes and questionable payments paid by American corporations. Dozens of business firms, many of them among the most prestigious and largest corporations in the country, have now been identified as having been involved in the international bribery system.

A DOUBLE STANDARD

Why do Americans think that they can apply one standard of ethics at home and a different one abroad, without damaging themselves and the views others have of them? We realize that our individual ethics apply not just within our own homes but also outside them. Why should we think that collectively as a nation we can disregard our ethical values when we go abroad?

Edwin O. Reischauer, "The Lessons of the Lockheed Scandal," **Newsweek**, May 10, 1976, p. 21.

The payment of foreign bribes is deplorable, inexcusable, and must be brought to a halt. Regardless of what is presumed to be the practice in any foreign country, and whether or not businesses from other countries engage in bribery, there is no excuse for an American to go into a foreign country and violate the laws of that country. Such practices are corrupt and morally wrong.

The bill I have introduced would be an effective way to put an end to these practices, so far as Americans are concerned, by requiring full disclosure of payments and by imposing criminal penalties on any American guilty of paying a bribe in a foreign country.

From time to time I intend to introduce into the **Record** evidence of the payment of bribes by business firms. The vast bulk of the evidence has so far been obtained by the Securities and Exchange Commission through its vigorous investigations and its voluntary disclosure program.

Today I will introduce documents provided to SEC by the General Tire & Rubber Co. At the request of SEC, General Tire began an investigation into alleged improper payments to employees of foreign governments in Chile, Morocco, and Rumania. The preliminary results of the investigation show a number of questionable transactions, including the following: First, that a foreign subsidiary of the company in an unnamed country maintained for many years a cash fund which was not recorded on the books of the foreign subsidiary. From 1969 to the fall of 1975 approximately $240,000 was paid from the fund and, according to the company:

> It appears that some payments made from this fund as well as other payments recorded on the subsidiary's books may have been improper or illegal payments to foreign government employees.

Second, another foreign subsidiary in another unnamed foreign country maintained U.S. dollar bank accounts in its name in the United States and England, as well as a local currency account in a local bank, none of which were recorded on the books of the foreign subsidiary. The company states that it has only limited information concerning the uses of those accounts, but

CAPITALISM AND CORRUPTION

Crusades against capitalism in areas where revolutionary changes are afoot have been greatly aided by the bribery, payoffs and graft revealed to be routine among large U.S. business corporations, particularly the multinationals. Especially the billions in U.S. arms sales put over on underdeveloped countries by huge pay-offs to crooked officials — usually with full knowledge of the Pentagon — have done incalculable harm to U.S. interests in Portugal, Italy, Greece and elsewhere, where public sentiments swing in the balance. Although greeted with a ho-hum in official Washington and Wall Street, what a tool we have handed to the Communisits! The last time the Kremlin caught a commissar taking bribes, they shot him. In Washington and Wall Street, he's often promoted.

Charles A. Wells, "Killing Capitalism," **Between The Lines**, August 1, 1975, p. 2.

has not yet disclosed what that limited information is. The company also states that the U.S. dollar accounts amounted to about $435,000 before they were closed out, and that they "appear to have violated the foreign currencies exchange controls of the country where the subsidiary was located."

The company concludes its disclosure by stating that the continuing investigation also includes the matter of political contributions in the United States and the degree of executive involvement in all the matters under investigation.

I request unanimous consent that the documents filed by the General Tire & Rubber Co. be printed in the **Record**.

NO LEGISLATION NEEDED FOR BRIBERY

William F. Buckley

William F. Buckley is the editor of the **National Review**. He has written many books and articles in support of conservative causes. He is one of the nation's leading conservative spokesmen.

Consider the following questions while reading:

1. For what reasons is Mr. Buckley against laws making it illegal to bribe foreign officials?
2. How does he distinguish between graft and corruption? Do you think this distinction is important?

William F. Buckley, ''A Law Against Bribes By Businessmen Abroad,'' **Minneapolis Tribune**, April 27, 1976, p. 7A. Reprinted with permission of the Washington Star Syndicate.

There is a movement to pass a law that could forbid U.S. corporations from tendering bribes or engaging in graft. Meanwhile, pressure increases on our own government, exerted by foreign governments, to release to them the names of all foreigners listed in congressional testimony as having received American money for illicit purposes. Concerning all this, a few observations:

• A request by a foreign government for names of indigenous politicians of easy morals is not necessarily sincere. There are two reasons for this. The first is that whatever the thirst for justice, there is the matter of national pride. Some countries would be depopulated if every official who had taken a bribe was exposed. Moreover, in some cases the people who are loudly demanding that the United States release the information are doing so in the way that some people sue splashily for libel: to distract attention from the fact of their own guilt.

The second is that it is very difficult to prosecute an official in the absence of evidence of his guilt. That evidence could hang on the credibility of an American businessman. Pray, how would a foreign government get that businessman to go over and testify in, say, a Peruvian court? What if, under local law, not only the Peruvian was a lawbreaker, but also the American? One would suppose that the relevant official, or ex-official, of Lockheed has enough problems without volunteering to go to jail in Peru for a few years.

• If we passed a law making it illegal to suborn a foreign official, American companies would, of course lose business to the extent that competitors were unburdened by similar laws, and proceeded to bribe their merry way into the good graces of foreign purchasers. Question: Would enterprising Americans feel that to protect their competitive position, they should penetrate the operations of foreign competitors in order to expose their corrupt practices? Would an American company be permitted to bribe an employee of a competitive company to report on the internal practices of that company? Or would the new law forbid this?

GRAFT AND CORRUPTION

• Herman Kahn of the Hudson Institute has often stressed the difference between "graft" and "corruption." I can find no etymological authority for that distinction, although it is eminently perceptible. Under the Kahn Rule, "corruption" is when you bribe the Mexican commissioner of motor vehicles to give you a driving license even though you are blind as a bat and are unable to distinguish Mexican democracy from authoritarianism.

"Graft" is when you give somebody in the office 100 pesos to give you your license, to which you are entitled, today, rather than three months from today, which is the normal bureaucratic pace. Graft (or whatever you wish to call it) is an anti-bureaucratic lubricant. Even so, it may be technically illegal. It is technically illegal for the networks to slip money into the hands of customs inspectors to persuade them not to open, and therefore delay delivery of, their precious cans of newsfilm, looking for smuggled dope. But if they failed to do so, it would leave John Chancellor at the mercy of Walter Cronkite, or vice versa. How would a law formulate the ethical distinction?

• And how would the law deal with the question of extortion? "Mr. Jones, sir, unless $100,000 is deposited in Swiss bank account Z 787-8 by next Monday, the minister of the interior will introduce legislation raising the tax on your refinery by 100 percent. If our calculations are correct, that will — er — drive you out of Nigeria."

It can't be done. It is strange that as our knowledge of cultural diversity increases, the old Wilsonian delusion that you can make everybody behave the way we want them to behave, survives. The boys are leading us toward a juridical Vietnam.

DISTINGUISHING BETWEEN STATEMENTS THAT ARE PROVABLE AND THOSE THAT ARE NOT

From various sources of information we are constantly confronted with statements and generalizations about social and moral problems. In order to think clearly about these problems, it is useful if one can make a basic distinction between statements for which evidence can be found, and other statements which cannot be verified because evidence is not available, or the issue is so controversial that it cannot be definitely proved. Students should constantly be aware that social studies texts and other information often contain statements of a controversial nature. The following exercise is designed to allow you to experiment with statements that are provable and those that are not.

In each of the following statements indicate whether you believe it is provable (P), too controversial to be proved to everyone's satisfaction (C), or unprovable because of the lack of evidence (U). Compare and discuss your results with your classmates.

    P = Provable
    C = Too Controversial
    U = Unprovable

_____ 1. The golden rule should be applied to all business activity and transactions.

_____ 2. The unemployment rate is over 70 percent for black youths between the ages of 16 and 21 in St. Louis.

_____ 3. There is a great deal of corruption in today's American business community.

_____ 4. Most businessmen are honest and more concerned about spiritual values than money and profits.

_____ 5. Businessmen are largely ignorant of the great spiritual and religious thinkers of the past.

_____ 6. Capitalism, competition and the profit motive have made the U.S. a free and wealthy society.

_____ 7. American business leaders are largely motivated by meaningless drives toward materialistic success.

_____ 8. It would be better if our society were organized around the principle of cooperation.

_____ 9. Inflation is higher this year than it was last year.

_____ 10. Our nation should follow a policy of rapid economic growth to avoid severe unemployment and economic discontent.

_____ 11. The major oil companies in America have formed what amounts to a monopoly in the oil industry.

_____ 12. Wage and price controls are needed to counter rapid inflation.

_____ 13. The federal government is preventing economic growth by over-regulation and intervention in the affairs of business.

CHAPTER 2

THE ROLE OF GOVERNMENT

BIG GOVERNMENT THREATENS FREEDOM

William E. Simon

William E. Simon became the 63rd Secretary of the Treasury in 1974. He was appointed by President Nixon and continued to serve under President Ford. As Secretary of the Treasury, Mr. Simon is the nation's chief financial officer, and chairs or holds membership on numerous national and international financial, trade and economic bodies.

Use the following questions to assist you in your reading:

1. What does the author say are some of the perils of big government?
2. How does the author say we can strengthen our economic vitality?
3. Can you relate the cartoon in this reading to the author's ideas?

William E. Simon, ''Big Government Or Freedom,'' **Vital Speeches**, April 15, 1975, pp. 386-89. Reprinted with permission from **Vital Speeches Of The Day**.

Frequently, those who support bigger government spending programs and greater governmental control over the economy are pictured as socially progressive, men and women of compassion who care about the problems of the little people. On the other hand, those who believe that the government does not have the ability to solve every problem and that instead we should be strengthening the free enterprise system are caricatured as a new generation of economic royalists who are indifferent to human suffering and care only about fattening the golden calf of big business.

These characterizations would mean little, except for the fact that they are so blatantly phoney. My experience in Washington has convinced me that almost every man and woman in a position of high public trust cares deeply about the welfare of our people, especially those who are impoverished or face disadvantages because of their sex or the color of their skin. The central question is not who cares the most, but how we restore our prosperity and reduce human hardships without sacrificing our freedom or destroying the most successful economic system that man has ever known.

I submit to you today that if America continues down the road toward greater governmental spending and greater governmental control over our economy — a road that we have been moving steadily down for several decades — then your generation will be robbed of your personal and economic freedoms and you will be condemned to an economy with chronic inflation and unemployment. That is really what's at issue in our economic debates, and those of you who are students have an even greater stake in the outcome than anyone in Washington today.

THE PERILS OF BIG GOVERNMENT

Let's look at a few facts about Government spending. For most of our history, a $100 billion Federal budget was like the four-minute mile in track: it was a limit that was never broken. Then in 1962, we finally went over the $100 billion mark — some 186 years after our Republic was founded. But we were not content to rest on our laurels, dubious though they were. Seven years later, the budget broke the $200 billion barrier, and then only four years later — this year, in fact — we are cracking the $300 billion mark. In the coming fiscal

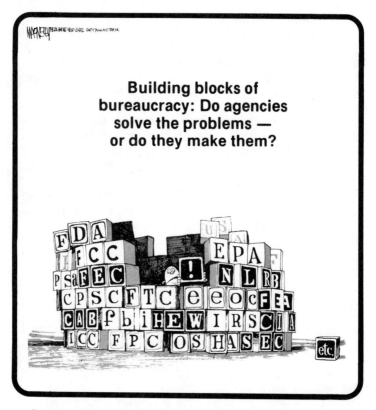

Building blocks of bureaucracy: Do agencies solve the problems — or do they make them?

Reprinted with permission from the Chicago Tribune-New York News Syndicate, Inc.

year, we are likely to go beyond $365 billion, so that the government will be spending $1 billion each and every day of the year....

As budgets grow, the Government comes to occupy a more and more dominant role within our society....

I submit to you when government grows that large, so that you have to give up perhaps half of your earnings to pay its bills, then you will have surrendered a substantial part of your freedom.

Nor should you think that you will necessarily be enlarging the freedoms of those you support with your taxes. As generous and concerned citizens, all of us have a responsibility to help less fortunate Americans. But the welfare system that we have imposed upon low-income people in this country is so riddled with inefficiencies and inequities that it not only wastes tax dollars but, more importantly, wastes the human potential of the poor. It is long past time that we overhauled our welfare system, replacing it with one that is fair, simple and genuinely compassionate.

For taxpayers, the burden of paying the Government's bills has become so heavy that many are ready to rebel against it. Last November, voters across the country turned down some three quarters of all bond issues on the ballot. Politicians realize this, of course, so that some of them will vote to increase spending and the next day will vote against higher taxes.

The result has been a string of Federal budget deficits that are unparalleled in our history. In 14 of the last 15 years, the budget has been in the red. As we approach the 1976 budget, we recognize that the effects of the recession will lower revenues and raise spending, thus enlarging the deficit. What we are confronting in 1976, however, is not a modest or even a large deficit but a monstrous one. If some members of the Congress prevail, our deficit for the coming fiscal year could exceed $80 or even $100 billion. Just imagine: fourteen years after the Federal Government broke the magic barrier of a $100 billion spending level, the deficit on the budget may actually grow to $100 billion....

Strengthening the Free Enterprise System

Still another result of the trend toward bigger government has been a definite slowing of our progress toward renewing and rebuilding the strength of our free enterprise system. Let me give you a concrete example of what is now happening. What financial analysts refer to as the "capital market" is really a pool of savings and other funds that are available for private investment. In the past, that pool has been the major source from which corporations have drawn when they want to invest in new plant and equipment. During the coming fiscal year, however, we estimate that government at all levels — Federal, State and local — will borrow between 80 to 85 percent of all new funds available in that investment pool. Less than one dollar out of every five in that capital market will be available for investment in private enterprise; the other four dollars will be gobbled up by the Government....

41

I know some of you may wince when we talk about profits. You may think they are already far too high for our own good. Actually, inflation has played tricks with corporate profits, so that some companies seem to be making more money than they actually are. Realistically measured, corporate profits have plunged by 50 percent over the course of the past 10 years. Last year, profits were so low that corporations had almost nothing to plow back into business, but had to dip into their capital reserves in order to make dividend payments. It is not unfair to say that we have been in a profits depression.

GROWING DANGER

My single overriding observation after these years in Washington is of the growing danger of an all-pervasive Federal government. Unless checked, that growth may take from us our most precious personal freedoms. It also threatens to shatter the foundations of our economic system.

Casper W. Weinberger, U.S. Secretary of H.E.W., before the Commonwealth Club of San Francisco, San Francisco, California, July 21, 1975.

Can the Government Do It Better?

How, then, do we restore our economic vitality?

One answer I hear with alarming frequency is that the Government should play a far more active role in regulating the economy. A poll commissioned by Time Magazine showed last week that 69 percent of our people want to revive wage and price controls. There are, indeed, areas in our economy where the public interest requires some form of government regulation. Few people question, for instance, that the nation's telephone system, which is inherently monopolistic, should be subject to public regulation. The growth of government regulation that we have witnessed in recent years, however, has exceeded all bounds of sensibility.

The 1973 automobile, for instance, was subject to 44 different government standards and regulations involving about 780 different tests that had to be met. As the chairman of a major automaker observed, "Government today has something to say about how we design our products, how we build them, how we test them, how we advertise them, how we sell them, how we warrant them, how we repair them, the compensation we pay our employees, and even the prices we may charge our customers."

And let us not delude ourselves about how well the Government can run something once it obtains control. It is no accident that three of the most economically troubled industries in the country today — railroads, airlines and utilities — are also among the most tightly regulated. Let me review a few examples of overzealous governmental regulation in action:

• It is almost twice as far from San Francisco to Los Angeles than from New York to Washington, and yet the air fare on the California trip is almost a third cheaper. Why? Because airlines operating intrastate in California are not controlled by Federal regulators....

I would suggest there is really no mystery about the way that we have dug ourselves into today's economic mess, nor is there any real doubt about the way to get out. Specifically:

— As we lift ourselves out of this recession, we must restore greater discipline to our fiscal and monetary affairs. Neither man nor government can afford to live beyond its means. Governor Landon, it might be remembered, first won national fame by slashing government spending and balancing the Kansas budget. He set an example for us all.

— Secondly, we must lift the deadening hand of government from the many areas of our economy such as energy where overzealous government regulations are now cramping our growth and our hopes for the future.

— Thirdly, we must begin to rebuild the economic foundations of our free enterprise system by making a dramatic shift away from policies that encourage consumption and spending and toward policies that encourage much greater savings, investment and capital formation. This is one of the greatest challenges of the next decade.

— Finally, we must awaken to the basic threat now posed to our liberties by the trend toward bigger and bigger government. This nation is still incredibly strong, solidly built on the foundation of personal and economic freedom, but we cannot long survive as a world leader if we continue to trade our freedoms to the Government in exchange for false promises of a better future.

In short, we must begin reordering our national priorities in a fundamentally different way. That is the best way — indeed, it is the only way — to provide a brighter future for all of the people of this country, rich and poor alike....

An epitaph written for the ancient city of Athens and attributed to the pen of historian Edward Gibbon is still relevant for us today. "In the end," he wrote, "more than they wanted freedom,they wanted security. They wanted a comfortable life and they lost it all — security, comfort and freedom. When the Athenians finally wanted not to give to society but for society to give to them, when the freedom they wished for most was freedom from responsibility, then Athens ceased to be free."

Whether the same will one day be said of America is the basic decision before us. It's really up to you and me to make sure this doesn't happen.

IN DEFENSE
OF BIG GOVERNMENT

Henry Fairlie

Henry Fairlie is an English journalist and is the author of **The Spoiled Child of the Western World** (Doubleday, 1976).

Keep the following questions in mind while reading:

1. Why does the author describe ''big government'' as a false issue?
2. What is the real issue facing Americans according to Fairlie?
3. What does he mean by the phrase ''Spoiled Child of the Western World?''
4. Why does the author say democracy has to acknowledge the gulf between rich and poor nations?

Henry Fairlie, ''In Defense of Big Government,'' **The New Republic**, March 13, 1976, pp. 24-27. Reprinted by permission of **The New Republic** © 1976, The New Republic, Inc.

There is something more than a little deceitful in a presidential candidate who tries to get to Washington by saying that he is running "against Washington," and hopes to be elected to the most powerful office in the world by proclaiming that he is against "big government." A saloon-keeper might as well justify his application for a license by saying that he is a member of the Temperance Reform League....

Too many of the "liberties" now being claimed from "big government" seem to me to be essentially "privileges" only for today's barons. It may be too much — it might even be wrong — for the Democratic party to begin this year to speak the language of socialism. But it is time that it was acknowledged that there are now only two choices: one can be either for *strong government for the few and the rich*, or for *strong government for the unrich and the many*. There is no longer a third way. This is what the American election this year is about: not whether there should be "big government" or not — that is a false issue — but whom the "big government" should serve.

The Democratic party must not, if it wishes to be true to its own tradition, and cannot, if it wants to win, appear to say "me too" to the conservative attacks on strong central government....

One of the difficulties is that much of the glibness comes from articulate men and women who are at least on the margins of the Democratic party, infesting its raiments. In response to the Vietnam war and to Watergate, they are recklessly careless of democracy's need for strong central government. They will believe nothing that the government says. Out of any mistake of the executive, they will bend their spite to prove malfeasance. They will not even allow the government to have its secrets. The work of government that is done by loyal and conscientious men, according to their own lights, earns from them hardly a sniff of regard. Having downgraded the work of Congress for 30 years, they suddenly find that virtue is encapsulated in the report of any congressional committee or subcommittee that chooses to seize some publicity by criticizing the government, no matter how flimsy the testimony on which the report is based, or how shallow its conclusions. Congressmen and senators who must have thought that they would end their careers in obscurity are now amazed and cheered to find that they can walk with their heads high, trailing clouds of glory, in the gutters of a press that believes them as credulously now as so recently it believed the President.

LET THE OLD ORDER DIE

Decision makers are not confronting the reality that the economy of the United States, as presently structured, is anti-people and anti-nature. It functions relatively smoothly for the interests of big capital, and brutally for the rest of us. Public policymakers must come to accept the fact that the old order is doing its best to die, and that we should let it.

Sam Love, "Let The Old Order Die," **The Progressive**, November, 1975, p. 41.

CORRECTIONS TO BE MADE

Of course there are corrections to be made in the working of the system; but one does not correct one's balance by turning a somersault, or repair an institution by tearing at its fabric. If the current mood continues much longer, thoughtless and unprincipled, America will soon have as heavy a price to pay for tearing at the fabric of government, as it had recently to pay for refusing to recognize that the fabric had been worn out of shape. I can hardly be accused, as an outsider, of having been slow to realize that the presidency had got out of hand. My first criticisms of the "Imperial presidency" were made 11 years ago, when it was not all that popular to make them. But to resist the pretensions of the presidency is not the same as repudiating the legitimate claims of government; and the Democratic party in particular should make the distinction....

Not for a hundred years has personal selfishness been so viciously presented as political prudence. What I have called "The Spoiled Child of the Western World" is not only American: he is all over the Western world, the child of "affluence," cunningly saying that all he wants is to be left alone to do "his own thing," and he will leave others alone to do "their own things," which of course means that he will leave them alone to be poor, to be uneducated, perhaps even to starve. If

47

there is one thing that India does not need today it is a shabby version of its own forms of spiritual passivity, yet the hippies journey to India with their degrading little visions, telling the Indians just to do "their own thing," while all the time, as an Indian said recently with contempt, for them there is always the check at American Express.

This seems to be not much worse than the boast of Karl Hess, the former assistant to Barry Goldwater, that he is a "full-time welder" — even a blacksmith — in the Appalachians! He is no more a "full-time" welder — or blacksmith — in any real sense than the hippie in India is in any real sense a follower of Krishna. For both there is the check at American Express, the passport out, whenever they wish to take it; and I find it objectionable for Hess to puff up his little haven of privilege in the Appalachians (while keeping his ties to the Institute for Policy Studies, of all places!), as if it is an answer for any but the privileged to the problems of modern technology and the "big" governments and corporations and unions which it demands.

But what do we expect of an assistant to Goldwater, except precisely this kind of selfish "libertarianism," as he loftily describes it....

There are other influences that can be traced, but my purpose here has solely been to show how the reaction against "big government," virtuous as it can be made to seem, is deeply related to the conservative reaction that has been building in the Western world for so long. For the sake of brevity, in what is no more than a shot across the bows in this election year, I will catalogue my main convictions:

MAIN CONVICTIONS

• Far from democracy's being the enemy of individual freedom in the modern age, as the "new conservatives" would have us believe, the extension of the democratic power is the only reliable defense of our liberties.

• Put in another way, this means that the extension of equality is now the only justification of our liberty.

• When the private power — of the barons, of the

corporations — is necessarily as great as it is in modern society, it can be checked only by a dynamic assertion of the public power. When a George Wallace attacks big government *and* big corporations *and* big unions with equal vehemence, one knows that the winner will be, whatever he says, the corporations.

• The scope of all power in the modern world is such that the scope of government is the most reliable of our resources. The central government needs to be not only strong and efficient but wide-ranging in its activities....

GOVERNMENT FOR THE FEW?

Too many of the "liberties" now being claimed from "big government" seem to me to be essentially "privileges" only for today's barons. It may be too much — it might even be wrong — for the Democratic party to begin this year to speak the language of socialism. But it is time that it was acknowledged that there are now only two choices: one can be either for strong government for the few and the rich, or for strong government for the unrich and the many.

Finally, if we may look out from that private welder's shop in Appalachia, democracy has to acknowledge that, one day soon, it is going to have to confront the ever-widening gulf between the poor nations and the rich nations. Oh! what a yawn comes from the "spoiled child." Yet it is ultimately by its ability to bridge that gulf that the future of democracy will be decided. It cannot be done by weak government, by small institutions, by village communes. Nothing goes to India from that welder's shop in Appalachia. If the actions of Indira Gandhi are shameful, she has at least this justification: that the great and prosperous democracies of the West have given no demonstration of the ability of their own governments to do it in any other way. When 400,000 new men, women and children arrive in New

Delhi every year, it is a little ridiculous and it is certainly deceitful to suggest that anything but "big government" can help.

And this points exactly to the kind of awkwardness with which the Democratic party is faced: that when there is a resistance to foreign adventures — as in Vietnam, as in Angola — that resistance all too easily topples over into a resistance to any foreign concerns at all. But with all the mistakes that it has made — and they have only been mistakes, they have not been wickednesses — the Democratic party in this century has searched to find the ways of avoiding so intolerable a contraction of the moral concerns of a great and free nation. It has been the most thoughtful, the most unprejudiced, the most tolerant, the most effective instrument of the democratic vision in the world. It has sought, intellectually and politically and morally, for the balance between liberty and equality, between authority and freedom, between action and unjustified interference. As I have said, there are now, as always, corrections in the balance to be made, but it will be a tragedy for untold millions in all parts of the world if the Democratic party surrenders even temporarily its conviction that strong government is necessary. And that a strong government not only can be free, but is the source of much of our new freedoms. The selfish "full-time" welder in Appalachia owes his privileges, not to the Republican party, but to the Democratic party, not to a narrow "libertarianism," but to a succoring democracy.

ECONOMIC PLANNING: AN OLD FALLACY

Milton Friedman

Milton Friedman is a prominent conservative economist. He has written many articles in scholarly and popular journals advocating conservative economic policies.

While reading use the following questions as a guide:

1. How does the author describe economic planning in Europe?
2. Why does he claim top down planning is inefficient?
3. Does the cartoon in this reading support what the author is saying?

We are suffering from inflation and recession produced by government attempts to promote full employment. Though it is now 21 months since the OPEC countries turned off the oil spigot, government still has no coherent plan to solve the resulting energy crisis. Postal service gets poorer and more expensive. The Interstate Commerce Commission has destroyed private railroad passenger travel and is well on its way to destroying private freight carriage. The Civil Aeronautics Board is performing a similar service for airlines. You can complete the litany.

The conclusion drawn by Senators Jacob Javits and Hubert Humphrey, encouraged by a recently formed Initiative Committee for National Economic Planning, is that the *private* economy has failed and must be reformed by establishing a new federal agency for economic planning — designed to operate without compulsion, relying instead solely on that infinite wisdom that government bureaucrats bring to every problem.

OLD FALLACIES

Apparently, old fallacies never die. Thirty years ago, "national economic planning" threatened to be the wave of the future. In Britain, the Labor Party's postwar victory over Winston Churchill spelled a commitment to central planning. In France, one proposed form of planning followed another through revolving governments. In the U.S., the Employment Act of 1946 rode the same wave. In British colonies heading toward independence, graduates of the London School of Economics spread the Fabian message of democratic socialism through central planning.

Friedrich Hayek's great polemic, **The Road to Serfdom**, was aimed at this wave. Dedicated to "socialists of all parties," its brilliant analysis of the defects of central planning and its demonstration of the tendency for such planning to destroy political freedom is as relevant today as then.

In any event, Hayek's fears proved fully justified. Wherever it was tried, central control of the economy was a failure. In Britain, successive versions of central planning have produced today's stagnation, raging inflation, and bitter internal divisions that threaten the

52

maintenance of British democracy. In the former colonies, central planning has stifled economic growth, produced widely shared misery, and undermined democratic institutions. India is the most tragic example.

"IF ONLY!!"

Reprinted with permission.

France's "indicative planning" was mostly talk — and France prospered. Germany rejected central planning, and, under Ludwig Erhard's guidance, moved in the opposite direction. The dramatic success of Germany's free-market economy reinforced the lesson of British failure.

What explains the failure of central planning? Can no planning be better than planning? That semantic trap confuses the real issue. The real issue is not planning vs. no planning, but what kind of planning, by whom, for what purpose.

ECONOMIC PLANNING

Unfortunately, the idea of national economic planning seems to have wide appeal. People usually respond sympathetically to the word planning, as in "planning a vacation," or "planning retirement." The meaning there is "to prepare for" — and, as every Boy Scout knows, to be prepared is good. But "planning" to the advocates of economic planning means more than preparation: it means an organized effort to direct, to control, to allocate the resources of a society — not according to the desires of freely-acting men and women — but instead to allocate resources in order to create a society according to the ideal of — guess who — the planners themselves.

From a speech by Thomas A. Murphy, Chairman, General Motors Corporation, delivered before the Greater Detroit Chamber of Commerce, Detroit, Michigan, June 5, 1975.

FOR US OR BY US?

The central planners want planning by them for us. They want the government — by which they really mean themselves — to decide "social priorities" (*i.e.* tell us what is good for us); "rationalize production" (*i.e.* tell us where and how we should work); assure "equitable distribution" (*i.e.* take from some of us to give to others of us). Of course, all this can be voluntary — if we are willing to turn our lives over to them. Otherwise, "antisocial behavior" must be restrained — who can gainsay that? The iron fist must be there — just in case.

Such planning, from top down, is inefficient because it makes it impossible to use the detailed knowledge shared among millions of individals. It undermines freedom because it requires people to obey orders rather than pursue their own interests.

I am for planning, too, but planning by each of us separately in light of our individual though shared, values, coordinated by voluntary exchange in free markets. Such planning, from the bottom up, enlists the interests of each in promoting the well-being of all. Government has its role — to provide a stable legal and monetary framework, enforce contracts, adjudicate disputes, and protect us from coercion by our fellow citizens. If we could limit government to these, its proper, functions, perhaps it could perform them successfully.

This is a plan too — a far better plan than establishing yet another federal agency to control our daily lives.

ECONOMIC PLANNING: A NECESSITY

Michael Harrington

Michael Harrington is the author of **The Other America** and is a Democratic Congressman from Massachusetts. He is the national chairman of the Democratic Socialist Organizing Committee.

Think of the following questions while you read:

1. How is capitalism defined by Michael Harrington?
2. Why does he say economic planning is a necessity?
3. What is "The Equal Opportunity and Full Employment Act" and why does the author favor it?
4. How do you interpret the cartoon in this reading?

Michael Harrington, "Jobs For All," **Commonweal**, January 30, 1976, pp. 73-77. Reprinted with permission from Commonweal Publishing Co., Inc.

National economic planning is now being placed on the political agenda. The reason is not hard to find. During the Kennedy-Johnson years, as Lyndon Johnson never tired of pointing out, there was the longest sustained boom in American peacetime history...

Now, a scant seven years since Johnson proclaimed in his final economic message to the Congress that economic life was no longer "a relentless tide of ups and downs" there have been nothing but ups and downs....

The workers and the poor have, as usual, borne the brunt of the disaster. Unemployment has soared to the highest levels in a generation — and if we used a realistic method of counting the jobless, those percentages would be double digit right now — and poverty, which declined modestly in the Sixties, is on the increase....

The planning now under discussion involves at the very most a structural transformation *within* the capitalist system. It is not, and will not be, radical. This means that the Left — the broad democratic Left as well as the smaller socialist Left in America — must approach the subject with considerable sophistication. Such a capitalist reform must not be rejected simply because it does not go far enough; but it must be supported in a way which pushes it to its Left limit and clearly states the necessity of going beyond that limit as soon as possible....

Capitalism, it must be stressed, is as a system hostile to full employment, and its periodic crises, insane as they are in any social calculus, are functional for such an economy. On the upswing, the system generates a capital goods boom, reduces unemployment and makes labor more militant as a consequence, which raises wages, bids up the price of money and allows marginal, inefficient producers to survive or even prosper. But at the height of a boom this prosperity becomes unbearable. Profits are cut by rising wages and other costs, investment tapers off and the capital goods industry turns down, and so on. Then comes the salvation of disaster. Mounting unemployment disciplines the labor force and reduces wages, the inefficient producers are driven out, the profit margins start up. The cycle can begin again....

Therefore if planning is going to begin to operate in a humane manner, it cannot be superimposed upon a fundamentally irrational and antisocial structure. The structure itself must be changed. Most fundamentally, the society has to begin to challenge the assumption that private profit and allocation must be the way to achieve growth. Specifically, an expansion of the area in which government — through public ownership, credit allocation, fiscal and monetary power — actually directs resources to decent use....

"AWW TOO BAD!"

Reprinted with permission from the **Guardian**.

A FULL EMPLOYMENT ACT

The "Equal Opportunity and Full Employment Act" — Hawkins-Humphrey — is much more of an immediate political possibility... Proposed by Augustus Hawkins, a very talented, hard-working Californian and a leading member of the Black Congressional Caucus, and Hubert Humphrey, it was stymied for a long time because the AFL-CIO refused to endorse it. Those disagreements are in the process of being ironed out right now (which means that some of the provisions I cite might change somewhat, but not the basic thrust of the Bill) and Carl Albert is said to have promised passage by this Spring. The chief feature of Hawkins-Humphrey is that, reverting to the concept urged by Franklin Roosevelt in 1944, it declares "that all adult Americans able and willing to work have the right to equal opportunities for useful paid employment at fair rates of compensation." The Employment Act of 1946 said that the citizen *should* have a job; Hawkins-Humphrey holds that he or she has a *right* to a job.

That right, everyone must realize by now, will not be spontaneously recognized by the private corporate economy. Among other things, it conflicts with the capitalist structural necessity of periods of joblessness. Therefore Hawkins-Humphrey rightly says that "it is the responsibility of the Federal Government to enforce this right...." The President is required under the act to make an annual report, revised after six months, which totals the amount of jobs estimated to result from the planned outlays of both the private and public sectors. "He or she" then determines the levels of expenditures, both public and private, needed to yield full employment. In the case of a shortfall the Job Guarantee Office under a newly renamed United States Full Employment Service would refer job-seekers for placement in a reservoir of projects, both public and private, drawn up by Local Planning Councils (which have already been set up under the Comprehensive Employment Training Act of 1973). In addition, there will be a Standby Job Corps which will enroll the unemployed for work on community public service projects. This would be regularly paid work at the minimum wage or better and compensation is required to be related to skill and also provide incentives to leave the Corps. I assume this last point means that the public employment cannot be as good as most private employment.

The most basic feature of Hawkins-Humphrey — the guaranteed right to a job — is such an enormous advance in American society that the bill should clearly be the focus of democratic Left efforts. But here again, those efforts should seek to transcend the overly-narrow limits in which this excellent idea is now constrained. Hawkins-Humphrey still fundamentally assumes that public employment is a kind of last resort. As Congressman Hawkins put it at hearings held in

59

1974 to introduce the bill, "The President is required to develop a national full employment and production program, covering all areas of economic activity, which is designed to promote sufficient employment opportunities through normal channels so that the activities of the U.S. Full Employment Service and the Standby Job Corps are reduced to a minimum." And he added a little later, "Priority is given to the development of jobs in the private sector."

Why? Can one really assume that Exxon has made a better use of resources, both human and material, than the TVA? Or that Penn-Central was more efficient than a nationalized rail system might have been? That it is better to over-build Florida condominiums and Nevada casinos while the housing of the poor rots? I need not answer such obviously rhetorical questions. Hawkins, whose work I very much admire in this area, is thereby making concessions to the ubiquitous mythology of a nation which pretends to be intensely practical: that Private is Good and Public is Bad. Of course, if you act on that proposition — for instance by giving the Post Office an impossible task and United Parcel Service an easy one — you can manufacture data to prove that it is true. The proponents of the bill may have felt required by political realities to stand in the center of the road; the democratic Left does not, and must not, do so....

NATIONAL PROJECTS NEEDED

Although the community control emphasis is absolutely essential and must be strengthened, it cannot be allowed to obscure the need for some truly national projects. A federal commitment to restore decent rail service through nationalized railroads operating in the context of a national transportation plan would be a marvelous device for generating a tremendous amount of employment, yet it cannot be planned or implemented at the community level (even though there must be community power over the local decisions about that rail network). Significant local participation is only possible in the framework of a national full employment policy; the latter can only be developed sensibly and democratically if there is the widest possible local participation. The federal and local functions should not be counterposed, even though they obviously will involve tensions. If full employment

60

planning is to work it must be composed of both....

Liberals can clearly support such proposals and Left liberals would do so enthusiastically. None of them requires that one declare for a basic socialist reorganization of society; all of them are located on the Left wing of possibility. The AFL-CIO and the UAW, for instance, are for various versions of most of these amendments. The compatibility of my suggestions with the best of the liberal tradition is, in a nation in which the mass Left goes no further than liberalism, an advantage to be welcomed by the socialist Left without the least embarrassment. But in joining the broad democratic Left to campaign for such measures, I think socialists have a unique job to do: constantly to demonstrate the necessity of going beyond the amelioration of a life in a basically flawed capitalist system as soon as possible. That means taking utterly seriously an ideal which liberals and socialists share, but which socialists follow to its basic conclusion: that economic power must be democratized throughout American society, that the age of corporate power, of an industrial feudalism in which tiny elites make fundamental and intolerable social choices on the basis of private profit, must now be brought to a close.

DISTINGUISHING FACT FROM OPINION

This discussion exercise is designed to promote experimentation with one's ability to distinguish between fact and opinion. It is a fact, for example, that the United States was militarily involved in the Vietnam War. But to say this involvement served the interests of world peace is an opinion or conclusion. Future historians will agree that American soldiers fought in Vietnam, but their interpretations about the causes and consequences of the war will probably vary greatly.

Some of the following statements are taken from readings in this book and some have other origins. Consider each statement carefully. Mark (O) for any statement you feel is an opinion or interpretation of the facts. Mark (F) for any statement you believe is fact. Then discuss and compare your judgments with those of other class members.

F = FACT   O = OPINION

_____ 1. We need a system of economic planning in the U.S.

✝ _____ 2. If America continues down the road of greater governmental spending, the coming generations will be robbed of their personal and economic freedoms.

✓ _____ 3. Large corporations, small businesses and private citizens all need big government.

_____ 4. We must acknowledge that big government is here to stay.

_____ 5. Americans are now suffering from both inflation and recession.

_____ 6. Most of our economic problems are products of government intervention into what was once a free economic system.

_____ 7. There are only two choices: one can be either for strong government for the few and the rich, or for strong government for the unrich and the many.

_____ 8. Only the power of a strong central government can check the private power and greed of the large corporate monopolies.

_____ 9. In Britain and other European countries, national economic planning has been a failure.

_____ 10. Central economic planning from the top down is inefficient because it undermines freedom by requiring people to obey orders rather than pursue their own interests.

_____ 11. Economic planning by the federal government is the only way to avoid chronic unemployment in our capitalistic economy.

_____ 12. Without central economic planning, large corporations will continue to pollute the environment and waste natural resources.

_____ 13. We must acknowledge that capitalism has been an economic system hostile to full employment.

_____ 14. The federal bureaucracy is not growing at an alarming rate since there are about the same number of federal employees now (5 million) as there were in 1961.

_____ 15. Of the 5 million federal employees, the overwhelming majority — 64 percent — work in just one huge agency: the Defense Department.

CHAPTER 3

BIG BUSINESS AND FREE ENTERPRISE

CONGLOMERATES EXPLOIT PEOPLE

Peoples Bicentennial Commission

> The Peoples Bicentennial Commission is an organization that is challenging economic concentrations of power. It believes that giant corporations have monopolies that threaten freedom, equality, and justice in America.

Use the following questions to help your understanding of the reading:

1. How are the abuses of large corporations described?
2. What is the message of the cartoon in this reading?
3. What economic changes are called for in the article?

Excerpted from a pamphlet published by the **Peoples Bicentennial Commission**.

Prudence, indeed, will dictate that economic systems long established should not be changed for light and transient causes; and accordingly all experience has shown that people are more disposed to suffer while evils are sufferable, than to right themselves by abolishing the forms to which they are accustomed.

But when a long train of abuses and usurpations, pursuing invariably the same object, evinces a design to reduce them under absolute despotism, it is their right, it is their duty, to throw off such economic institutions and to provide new guards for their future security. Such has been the patient suffering of the American People; and such is now the necessity which compels us to alter our former economic system. The History of the present giant corporations is a History of repeated injuries and usurpations; all having in direct object the establishment of an absolute tyranny over these States. To prove this, let the facts be submitted to a candid World.

America's Giant Corporations have seized control over the great land and resources of our country.

They have systematically destroyed thousands of small businesses and forced millions of Americans to become wage serfs for the wealthy owners.

PERMANENT INFLATION

Inflation, which will approach or even surpass an annual 10% rate, has now become a permanent feature of U.S. monopoly capitalism. Over the past decade, for instance, consumer prices have soared upward 72%. Wholesale prices have skyrocketed an even higher 83%. The steepest jumps have come in the last three years and virtually every economic forecaster sees a permanent annual inflationary increase from 6% to 8% for the foreseeable future.

Irwin Silber, "Has Economy Recovered?" **Guardian**, October 1, 1975, p. 1-2.

They have formed shared monopolies in virtually every major retail and wholesale industry, forcing millions of consumers to pay higher and higher prices for goods and services they cannot do without — these monopoly practices being the primary cause of runaway inflation.

They have forced millions of Americans into unemployment lines by systematically closing down their American plants and moving their business operations abroad so they can hire cheaper labor and reap still greater profits for their owners.

In the name of profit, they have expropriated billions of dollars of wealth produced by the working women and men of this country.

The Giant Corporations have:

Pursued a policy of industrial negligence which kills 14,000 workers and permanently disables 900,000 more every year.

They have manufactured unsafe products that kill 30,000 and permanently disable 110,000 Americans each year.

They have used the energy crisis in order to double the price of fuel and make record gains in profit.

They have sold American wheat to the Russian Government, forcing a sharp rise in the cost of bread and other wheat products to the American consumer.

They have turned our Nation into a weapons factory, wasting valuable labor and resources that could be utilized for basic human needs.

They have fostered tensions and conflicts between races, sexes and ethnic groups in their arbitrary and discriminatory employment practices.

They have pillaged the resources, exploited the peoples, and systematically intervened in the domestic affairs of other nations in order to profit their corporate treasuries.

The Giant Corporations have subverted the Consti-

tution of the United States and the principle of Government of, by, and for the people:

By illegally financing their own candidates for local, state and national office.

By placing their own supporters in key government commissions and regulatory agencies.

By using massive lobbying operations to virtually dictate the legislative direction of the State and Federal Governments, including the decisions on how our tax money is to be allocated.

MONOPOLISTIC DEVICES

Expansionary industries are largely dominated by giant corporations; in recessionary times, or during booming inflations, even in our modern stagflation, they can use monopolistic devices to preserve their prices and profits. Indeed, hard times help them knock out competition and discipline the labor force.

David Bensman and Luther Carpenter, "Dead End Of An Ideology," **The Nation**, November 8, 1975, p. 457.

It is these same Corporate Giants:

That profess the strongest attachment to self-reliance, while pocketing billions of dollars of our tax money in the form of Government subsidies and special favors.

That profess their commitment to preserving their country's future, while systematically destroying our natural environment.

That herald the virtues of personal responsibility and accountability, while engaging in wholesale crime under the protection of their corporate charters.

Reprinted with permission from **The Daily World**.

America's giant corporations have issued a death sentence against the individual human spirit:

By forcing millions of Americans to perform mindless functions eight hours per day inside the corporate machine.

By rewarding obedience, conformity, and dependency — and penalizing creative thinking, criticism, and independent judgment.

Corporate Giants have violated our sacred rights to life, liberty and the pursuit of happiness:

By denying us adequate access to the means to sustain life.

By severely limiting our opportunities to choose the kind of work life we would like to lead.

By denying us a range of work choices that are potentially self-fulfilling and rewarding.

The corporations have created and perpetuated a small hereditary aristocracy, with wealth and power unrivaled in the annals of recorded history.

The Corporate System has proven itself to be grossly inefficient and wasteful, while the Corporate owners and managers have proven themselves to be incompetent to make prudent decisions that effect the economic well-being of the American people.

In their obsession with profits, their lust for absolute dominion over the life of this Nation, and their total disregard for the American people, Corporate owners and managers have plunged our country into its present state of economic chaos, destroyed the lives of millions of families, and threatened the very survival of the Republic.

In every stage of these oppressions, we have petitioned for redress in the most humble terms: Our repeated petitions have been answered only by repeated injury. An economic system, whose character is thus marked by every act which may define an absolute tyranny, is unfit to claim the loyalty and allegiance of a free and democratic people.

We, therefore, the Citizens of the United States of America, hereby call for the abolition of these giant institutions of tyranny and the establishment of new economic enterprises with new laws and safeguards to provide for the equal and democratic participation of all American Citizens in the economic decisions that effect the well-being of our families, our communities, and our Nation. In furtherance of our joint hopes and aspirations, and mindful of the lessons of History, we steadfastly adhere to the general principle that a democratic Republic can only exist to the extent that economic decision-making power is broadly exercised by the people and not delegated to a few. Such is the necessity which compels us to act in support of decentralized economic enterprises, with ownership and control being shared jointly by the workers in the plants and by the local communities in which they operate — with similar patterns of shared representative control being exercised on a regional and National level to insure the smooth and efficient coordination of all economic operations. For the support of this Declaration, with a firm reliance on the protection of Divine Providence, we mutually pledge our lives, our fortunes, and our sacred honor.

IN DEFENSE OF LARGE CORPORATIONS

Melvin D. Barger

Melvin D. Barger is director of corporate communications for the Libbey-Ownes-Ford Company. The following reading was originally delivered as a speech to the Toledo Lions Club on March 11, 1976.

Use the following questions to assist you while reading:

1. What are the three main problems facing big business, in the author's opinion?
2. According to the author, why do we need big corporations?
3. What kind of economic future does he predict?

It is common knowledge that Big Business is in trouble with the public, and of course my work in corporate communications makes me constantly and painfully aware of this fact. All of the public opinion polls show results that are unfavorable to business. This anti-business trend has been noticeable for a long time. More than 20 years ago, I began attending meetings and seminars that were devoted to giving the public a better understanding of business. Evidently we haven't done a good job, because business — particularly Big Business — has become everybody's favorite villain. Big Business is the villain in television shows, the villain in the supermarket, the villain on the campus, and the *arch*-villain in legislative and government circles....

It is probably necessary to point out that most criticism is aimed at *Big* Business and there's still some sympathy for the small business firm or the smaller corporation. But this should bring little comfort to the smaller business firm, because every business is related to Big Business operations and gets involved in the same kinds of problems that are facing the large companies. Communities have a stake in this too, because large companies are part of their economic life. Here in Toledo, for example, we have seven locally-headquartered companies that are listed in **Fortune** magazine's directory of the 500 largest industrial corporations. We also have large plants owned by other **Fortune** "500" companies. Anything that affects Big Business for good or ill will also affect us and our community.

My own bias is that I do not think Bigness is necessarily Badness. Yet I can't remember a time when the term *Big Business* did not cause bad vibes in the public mind. I also believe in private property, a free marketplace, and individual liberties. I do not believe that the answer to all human problems can be found in Washington, D.C., and I am frankly apprehensive about the road ahead.

THE PLIGHT OF LARGE CORPORATIONS

What is the plight of the large corporations? In my opinion, the corporation has at least three major problems. *One is the point I've been making, that Big Business is not loved.* Big Business is hated and feared

73

by large groups of people and for a variety of reasons. There always has been a strain of anti-business bias in America; now it is active, influential, well-organized and militant.

The second problem is that the corporation is rapidly losing ground in running confrontations with consumerists, environmentalists, ecologists, and other cause movements. Maybe all of these causes are good. For the corporation, however, they are bringing a burden of regulations and controls that are destroying not only its vitality and flexibility, but also its ability to solve problems. Most of these regulations are manageable when taken separately. Cumulatively they are becoming a millstone that is slowly crushing some companies and industries to death.

The third problem is that the corporation is poorly defended and supported in the political arena. Two years ago, Professor Irving Kristol of New York University pointed out in a **Wall Street Journal** article that the corporation has no political constituency. He said that "the corporation today is largely defenseless — a nice, big, fat, juicy target for every ambitious politician, and a most convenient scapegoat for every variety of organized discontent." Hostility toward the large corporation is not new, he pointed out, but what IS new is the corporation's utter defenselessness against this hostility. There (the corporation) is, he says, a wealthy and powerful institution that is utterly vulnerable to a political take-over bid. Naturally, the competition is keen. And whatever the powers and resources are that enable the corporation to succeed so well in the marketplace, they don't work down in Washington. There's small wonder that the large corporation may, as Professor Kristol said in another article, look more and more like a species of dinosaur on its lumbering way to extinction. "The cultural and political environment becomes ever more hostile; natural adaptation becomes ever more difficult; possible modes of survival seem to be beyond its imaginative capacity."

At this point, perhaps the proper remarks are "So the corporation is a dinosaur on its way to extinction. Who cares? If the corporate dinosaur can't survive in the new environment, maybe it doesn't deserve to. What difference will it make in our lives, anyhow, if the dinosaur dies?"

WHY WE NEED BIG CORPORATIONS

There are several good reasons why we need the Big Corporation. For one thing, we will continue to require the goods and services of Big Business. Producing and marketing goods and services at market prices is the businessman's thing, something that he does with the skill and ease of a Jack Nicklaus playing golf. This job has been done so well that we've taken it for granted. We may think that the goods and services will flow forever no matter what we do to the business system. The truth is that the current attacks on the business system will profoundly inhibit the Big Corporation's long term ability to provide goods and services at acceptable prices. We have already seen some effects of this punitive campaign, and there's much more on the road ahead if we follow our present course. Every regulation and restriction carries a price tag — and you and I must pay that price.

We also need the corporation as the efficient manager of resources, labor services and capital. Here again, it's the Jack Nicklaus thing. Private corporations have, on balance, performed so well in bringing together resources and capital that we don't pause to consider how badly this job is botched when it's done by the wrong people operating under different ground rules.

The large corporation also serves as an instrument of material progress, although it gets little credit for this service. I am thinking here of improvements in materials, manufacturing methods, distribution, and products. True, companies did not give us these benefits out of the goodness of their hearts; market forces required them to improve or die. But if we don't have the big company around to bring new products and ideas on stream, the job just won't be done. There's nobody out there to do it....

And that's a fourth reason for sticking with the big, privately-owned corporation: It's really the only game in town. Nobody has an alternate system that works. We seem to be heading toward some kind of socialism, but if we ever get there, we won't like it and we won't be able to make it work without banging a lot of heads together.

What about a mixed economy, with cooperative ventures between Business and Government? Well, we already have that to a large extent, and it's an unstable mixture. What it really means is that some businesses eventually become wards of the Government. The railroads were the first large industry to become a mixed economy, and were badly crippled long before we had the Penn Central mess. We don't know what the railroads would be like today if they had been left alone, but it's hard to believe that a country possessing so many dynamic and thriving industries couldn't also have had progressive and profitable railroads.

Finally, we need Big Business because it still gives us freedom of choice in the marketplace. That freedom of choice is another thing we take for granted. It won't always be there if we continue on the present course. We are already paying for many things that we wouldn't buy if we were given free choice in the matter. You can still choose among makes of automobiles, TV sets, suits of clothes, and canned goods. You have no choice in the matter when your money is spent on countless Federal ventures that will not benefit you or your community. I am sometimes told that we voted for these programs. I don't remember doing any such thing; I think we simply lost freedom of choice in these matters.

THE PRESENT TRACK

What will happen to Big Business and the American economy if we continue on the present track? Ever since the advent of the New Deal, businessmen have been saying that various Federal measures and programs would bring about collapse or dictatorship. I don't think we'll have either. What we will probably get is stagnation and a great deal of bureaucratic control. We probably *won't* get brownshirts marching in the streets and hauling people off in the middle of the night for torture and questioning. We *will* get a great deal of humiliating and exasperating controls from the various bureaus and agencies that now rule our lives in so many ways. We will pay, and pay again for the kind of bureaucratic foolishness that we joke about in our daily conversation. This is not scare talk. The American alternative to private, profit-seeking business is a whole system of Government-controlled, Government-subsidized, and Government-regulated businesses. This *must* result in an unresponsive marketplace, marked by frequent shortages and costly surpluses.

The model for this future American society is Great Britain, not the Soviet Union. The reports from Britain nowadays are grim; they tell of a once-great nation that is sliding into stagnation and decay. The distinguished journalist Vermont Royster was a recent visitor to Britain who sees a parallel between what happened in Britain and what is happening here. Surprisingly, good intentions, not bad ones, got the British into trouble. It began with the most humanitarian motives, first the desire to provide free health care to all, and then the addition of subsidies for food and housing. Actually, a good society *should* be able to subsidize some of its parts, particularly people in need, and neither I nor Mr. Royster would argue with that objective.

What happened, however, was that the British government eventually was forced to subsidize auto manufacturers, steel mills, shipyards, and coal mines; that is to say, Mr. Royster writes, many of the parts of the economy which should be not only self-supporting but providing a surplus for subsidizing the health program and the like, these parts are themselves subsidized. Well, we know what happened. A sticking point was reached that plunged the whole country into trouble. Here in the United States, we haven't reached that sticking point, but we're trying hard. I find it ominous when our Government begins to subsidize certain industries, because here, as in Britain, it is the profit-seeking part of our economy that should always support the parts we choose to subsidize.

It is not chance or accident or even poor management that converts corporations from profit-making institutions into wards of the state. It is really almost inevitable that companies drift into this kind of dependency once they become subject to political intervention. First, the state intervenes in the affairs of an industry and takes over critical decision-making powers. Before long, most of the firm's decisions are made in response to political pressures rather than market forces, though it manages to remain profitable in the short run. In the next phase, however, the company begins to lose money. But since the company is large and important, political pressure causes the government to step in to save it with subsidies. This

77

sets a precedent for other companies in similar trouble, and before long the state has a glut of subsidized industries....

One doesn't have to be an economist to understand that this is an undesirable result and that it cannot work indefinitely; there has to be a sticking point.

I believe that most business leaders perceive these dangers and oppose government intervention for fairly honest reasons. There are others, however, who march down to Washington to demand subsidies for their own industries or legislation that will give them an advantage over their competitors. Unfortunately business today is divided on many questions at the very time it faces its most serious threat....

There has also been some interest in building a political constituency for the corporation, thanks to the article by Mr. Kristol. Chief executive officers of major corporations have referred to this need, but so far nobody's shown how a corporate constituency can be put together. And without a constituency, the corporation continues to lumber along on its way to extinction, a nice, big, fat, juicy target for everybody.

Well, who are to be the constituents of Big Business? Professor Kristol thought that shareholders could do this job, if they could be brought into a more active role. This suggestion has merit, but shareholders have been strangely silent about harsh political action that harms their equity holdings. I'm afraid that many shareholders think of their stock as an investment and not a cause and will not take the time to go to bat for Big Business in general.

Union members and salaried employees of companies could also be corporate constituents. The difficulty here is that many employees hold inconsistent views. They want job security and good pay and benefits, and may even think well of their own company. But they may also be hostile toward Big Business in general and may even support actions that will eventually come home to roost right where they work. They are not to be criticized for this inconsistency; it is almost impossible to show, until it is too late, that attacks on Big Business are a threat to the employee's own job security. A company's plant communities often

78

share that attitude; they like the companies in their city but they want to see the other guys punished.

I haven't by any means given up hope. Probably the real corporate constituency is not to be found in any special interest group. It has to be found among all groups; it has to be found among the responsible people with common sense who know that in the long run there's no such thing as a free lunch. The common sense people, if given all the facts bearing on a problem, can usually be counted on to make judgements that are fair, reasonable, and consistent. Common sense people can be critical of certain corporate actions without calling for the end of the competitive enterprise system. Common sense people certainly know that their own economic wellbeing is made more secure by the success and growth of large business firms; they also know that any cost burden or restriction imposed on business eventually finds its way to the customer, the employee or the shareholders. They know that we need the Big Corporation, not as a subsidized and sickly ward of the government, but as a healthy, independent, and progressive institution in society.

READING 13

CAPITALISM FOR THE POOR AND SOCIALISM FOR THE RICH

Sidney Lens

Sidney Lens, an activist in radical, labor, and peace movements, has written extensively on domestic and international issues. His most recent book is **The Promise and Pitfalls of Revolution**, published by the United Church Press.

Use the following questions to help your understanding of the reading:

1. What does Sidney Lens mean by the phrase "socialism for the rich"?
2. What examples does he give of "socialism for the rich"?
3. According to Lens, why is corporate socialism now in decline?
4. How does the cartoon relate to the reading?

Sidney Lens, "Socialism for the Rich," **The Progressive**, September, 1975, pp. 13-19. Reprinted with permission from **The Progressive**, 408 West Gorham Street, Madison, Wisconsin 53703, Copyright © 1975, The Progressive, Inc.

When Trans World Airlines ran into heavy economic storms recently — allegedly because of higher fuel prices — it had no qualms about petitioning the Civil Aeronautics Board for a $184.1 million subsidy. TWA saw nothing subversive in a free-enterprise corporation appearing before government with a tin cup. Such incidents have, in fact, become commonplace, and the tin cups are engraved with the names of such giants as Lockheed, Penn Central, Pan American, and many others....

But necessary as it may be under our present value system for government to fill corporate tin cups, there is something inconsistent about it: It does not jibe with Bicentennial boasts about the glories of "free" enterprise, "free" markets, and "laissez faire."...

This is not what Adam Smith meant by "laissez faire (leave alone) capitalism" when he published his monumental work, **The Wealth of Nations**, in 1776. When the burden of risk is placed on government, we no longer have free enterprise; we have a bastardized system that may properly be called "corporate socialism."

A few years ago, Lockheed, the nation's largest military contractor, and Penn Central, the nation's largest railroad, asked Congress to guarantee bank loans of $250 million and $200 million respectively. Congress, in its capricious wisdom, approved Lockheed's request but turned down Penn Central (for the time being). Many concluded from this that government aid to corporations was random and insignificant. They could not have been more wrong. At that very moment the Federal Government had outstanding some $56 billion in direct loans, as well as $167 billion in loan guarantees, or a total of $224 billion — twice the sum of all commercial and industrial loans that commercial banks had outstanding at that time. The bankers, who preach "free enterprise" on Sunday but are queasy about it Monday through Friday, evidently are not keen on taking risks....

TWO WELFARE SYSTEMS

As economist Paul A. Samuelson observes, "Each period of emergency — each war, each depression — expands the activity of government." During the World War I emergency, Washington temporarily operated the rail industry, rationed primary goods, effectively curtailed the right to strike, and floated $25 billion in Liberty bonds. After the war, the Government eased itself out of most of these economic functions, but the Great Depression that began a decade later qualitatively changed the role of government — especially after Franklin D. Roosevelt took the reins. The Government began to operate two parallel welfare states — one symbolized by relief for the poor, makeshift Federal jobs, Social Security, and unemployment compensation, and the other by the Reconstruction Finance Corporation and dozens of "pump priming" measures.

Both the welfare state for the poor and the less publicized welfare state for the rich were conceived as temporary expedients to be dismantled, at least in part, when conditions returned to "normalcy." But since 1929 the nation has not seen a single day of normalcy, and the two welfare states not only have been vastly extended but institutionalized. Their growth testifies to the fragile nature of the nation's economic-political structure.

The welfare state for the poor is indispensable as a cushion against social turmoil. Cut off the Social Security and retirement payments that go to more than thirty million elderly, the unemployment payments to six million (or more) jobless, the billions of dollars spent for fifteen to eighteen million Americans on welfare, and this nation would be a cauldron of seething discontent, not far from revolution.

The welfare state serving business and the affluent is indispensable to keep the present economic system in operation. It is obviously far more generous than the welfare state that serves the poor. For example, Brookings economists Joseph Pechman and Benjamin Okner have estimated that the benefits of the capital gains tax alone adds $13.7 billion a year to the incomes of the relatively small number of people who invest in stocks. And Philip M. Stern estimated in 1972 that "various exceptions and preferences embedded in the nation's tax laws" provided a bonus of $77 billion for the middle and upper classes — many times the amount allocated to the millions on public welfare.

Even more significant than such back-door handouts

to individuals, however, are the direct and indirect subsidies to many industries which otherwise would have to be curtailed, put in mothballs, or totally re-shaped....

"The system of free enterprise...has fired the imagination and determination of our people."
—Sec. William Simon

"The system of free enterprise...has fired the imagination and deter-mination of our people" ---Sec. William Simon
— copyright 1975 by Herblock in **The Washington Post**.

TODAY'S CAPITALISM

The goal of today's capitalism is to pass more and more of the risk to government by socializing normal business expenses (as in the maritime industry), or by socializing losses (as in the passenger rail industry). Either way, there is ample confirmation for the old adage that "socialism" is when the Government gives money to the poor, "capitalism" is when it gives it to the rich.

Business and government still use the rhetoric of laissez faire, but they can't really mean it....

On May 1, 1971 — appropriately, a revolutionary holiday all over the world — a quasi-public corporation, Amtrak, took over operations of intercity passenger service, and the carriers were off the hook. Not only were they relieved of previous losses, they were guaranteed an operating profit to run their old passenger trains (and a few new ones) under the Amtrak emblem. They now are reimbursed for all their direct costs, plus some overhead expenses, plus a 5 per cent assured profit. Amtrak, meanwhile, is losing heavily ($153 million in the first full year, 1972) and comes to Congress every year for ever larger sums.

If the Government had nationalized the *whole* railroad industry, losses in passenger service would have easily been compensated by the profits in the freight part of the industry — but that is not how corporate socialism works. Volpe and Nixon, abetted by such liberals as Senator Vance Hartke of Indiana, arranged it so that only the losing part of the business was made a government responsibility; the profitable part is still in private hands.

If government can socialize losses, why doesn't it socialize profits? If it can nationalize intercity passenger service, why not the highly profitable oil industry or the banks? If the Government takes the risk, why shouldn't *it*, rather than private interests, also take the reward? In other words, if we can have corporate socialism for the rich, why not public socialism? Since there is no longer a choice, in any case, between laissez faire capitalism and socialism, but only between private or public socialism, why not opt for the real thing?

CORPORATE SOCIALISM

Corporate socialism bases itself on the old Herbert Hoover "trickle-down" theory, which holds that if a capitalist is given the incentive in the form of potential profits, he will produce more wealth, the benefits of which will somehow "percolate" down to the lower classes in a continuing spiral of prosperity. Louis Menk of Burlington Northern implies that if management is allowed to manage it can produce wonders. In fact, however, management has been unable to manage since 1930 without state subsidy and state direction of the economy. Private capitalism is a failure, for if the state had not intervened — and continued to intervene on an ever larger scale for the last forty years — the capitalist system would have died long ago. Good management may have contributed to the prosperity of 1940-1971, but it was the Government's expenditure of $1.25 trillion on the military in that period, and innumerable billions in subsidies to private business, that really promoted prosperity....

Though corporate socialism worked for a while — mainly by borrowing against the future and by exploiting people in the underdeveloped nations — it is now obviously in decline. Living standards are no longer rising but falling, and a new cycle of "immiseration" of the lower classes is under way.

Corporate socialism has failed to solve its endemic problem of mounting surpluses, and is unable to contain world revolution. Those problems are, in fact, becoming more acute, leading inevitably to trade wars, money wars, "little" wars (with "tactical" nuclear weapons) against nationalist revolutionaries, and the ultimate catastrophe of total nuclear incineration.

Corporation socialism has, paradoxically, enhanced the power of big business and weakened that of the populace at large. One would assume that with the Government so deeply entrenched in economic matters, and business so dependent on government, the corporate goliaths would be subordinate. But in fact — as Richard J. Barnet and Ronald E. Muller have shown in their recent book, **Global Reach** — the multinational firm and the conglomerate enjoy much greater control over government than ever before. They have effectively eviscerated most of what remains of "government by consent of the governed" and reduced the countervailing power of the lower classes to a vanishing shadow. Thus, state management of the economy and a militarist foreign policy lead us not to happier days but toward a full-fledged totalitarianism.

Corporate socialism misdirects the economy into dead ends and titanic waste. Private profit and social responsibility clearly do not mix; on the contrary, the emphasis on profit maximization necessarily warps the economy in the direction of those industries and interests that have the biggest "clout." In recent decades, for example, the automobile and truck have become the linchpins of our economy, to the detriment of mass transit and the railroads. The Government has spent mountains of money on the interstate highway system, encouraging the substitution of autos and trucks for railroads and local mass transit. From a social perspective, this is disaster.

A fully loaded freight train uses only a quarter of the fuel that trucks do per ton-mile — and does not pollute the atmosphere to nearly the same extent. One track, says Anthony Haswell, chairman of the National Association of Railroad Passengers, can handle as much human traffic as ten to twenty lanes of expressway. Yet the funding for highways far exceeds aid to railroads, thereby wasting our shrinking energy resources, further befouling the atmosphere, and abetting the deterioration of inner cities as the middle classes flee to the suburbs on expensive expressways. The economy is also misdirected by expenditure of so great a proportion of our resources on the military, while such social needs as health care and housing remain unmet.

In its current "maturity," corporate socialism is a one-way ticket to perverted social priorities, permanent economic crisis, internal dictatorship, and war. The moral justification for free enterprise — that it guaranteed prosperity, peace, and democracy — was never solidly founded, but at least it was credible as a theory. There is no such moral justification for corporate socialism, even in theory — as "libertarian" advocates of free enterprise and right-wing Republicans correctly point out. If government is to be the risk-taker of last resort, then government, as the presumed representative of *all* the people, should take its risks in the public interest, not in behalf of private interests.

The choice for the United States in the 1970s is no longer between a free enterprise capitalism that exists only in the dark recesses of Ronald Reagan's imagination, and socialism. The choice is between corporate socialism and true, participatory socialism. Time — and moral justification — ran out on laissez faire capitalism in the 1930's. Time — and moral justification — are running out on corporate socialism now.

PROFITS PROMOTE SOCIAL WELFARE

Harold J. Cummings

Harold J. Cummings is Chairman-Emeritus of the Minnesota Mutual Life Insurance Company. He prepared this article with the help of John J. Verstraete Jr., Vice President of the 3M Company, and Roger E. Larson, Vice President of the Minnesota Mutual Life Insurance Company.

Consider the following questions while reading:

1. According to the author, how much money did American business devote to social purposes?
2. How does he say profits are important to all Americans?
3. What examples does the author give of social contributions made by American business?

Harold J. Cummings, ''The Crucial Role of Profits in American Society,'' **Human Events**, February 21, 1976, pp. 10-12. Reprinted with permission.

"Why shouldn't business devote its profits to 'social purposes'?"

The above block-buster exploded at an afternoon meeting of about 500 college presidents, high school principals, professors, teachers and graduate students — grouped at tables of eight — all eager to explore how American business might help in the solution of community problems. Each group had been invited to address one question to the podium, where four businessmen were ready to answer.

This astonishing query continues to come up, even from some businessmen and economists who should know better. Are they unaware that in 1973, a typical year, American business devoted somewhere between one-half and three-quarters of its earnings to "social purposes"? And that in 1973 stockholders were left with 17 per cent — less than one-fifth of *total earnings*?

• American business devoted $2 to "social purposes" from *pre-tax* earnings alone, vis-a-vis each $1 paid to stockholders out of *after-tax* profits; and that

• Including the income taxes paid by individual stockholders, the ratio was almost $3 for "social purposes" for every $1 for stockholders; and that

• If reinvestment of earnings in plant and equipment, to maintain today's jobs now, and to create new jobs for tomorrow serves a "social purpose," the ratio approaches $5 for "social purposes" for every $1 left stockholders; and that

• In any case stockholders were left with less than one-fifth of total earnings — just 17 per cent — for dividends!

Do even educators, not just the general public, have a polluted picture of "business," "earnings" and profits"?

"Profit" is not a four-letter word. Profit is not a dirty word, either. Profit — business profits — are the indispensable catalyst without which the American economic system just would not work! Nothing less!

Let's spell it all out.

DEFINING PROFITS

Long ago Alexander Hamilton Business Institute defined business as the process of *investing money* at a *hazard* in the *hope* of a *profit*. And do note the key words "hazard" and "hope." If there's no *money* invested, no *hazard* of loss, and no *hope* of a profit — it isn't business.

Profit is that something hoped for by an entrepreneur — some venturesome fellow — who gets an idea for a brand-new product. In the "hope" of a profit, he decides to "hazard" his lifetime savings — or to borrow capital and pay interest — to bring his dream out to the market place. He goes into business!

So

• He buys or leases a piece of land.

• He buys or builds a shop or a factory.

• He selects and pays for the raw materials going into the product.

• He designs and installs the needed machinery.

• He hires employes, starts paying salaries and fringe benefits.

• He selects and trains a sales force.

• He provides all the collateral necessities: advertising, insurance and what not — and finally

• He starts the production wheels rolling, hoping to get his vision out on the market place at a price that will sell and give him a "profit," before that inevitable competitor comes up with something better! Or cheaper! Or both!

By this time he will have learned the meaning of "hazard" and "hope."

He worries through all this knowing that, even if he should come out with a potential profit, government will step in forthwith and preempt about half for "social purposes."

But even then our bold entrepreneur may not have any "profit."

You see, he knows that buildings will deteriorate and machines will wear out. So he must start setting up a depreciation fund, hopefully in sufficient amount to maintain the plant and keep him in business.

Then, too, knowing that emergencies will surely occur, he must build up an adequate surplus — just as every family should have three to six months emergency money in a savings account.

And because he must keep continuously abreast of the challenging changes in the market place — new products, competitive promotions, economic fluctuations, prices, costs, laws, customers — he must invest substantial sums in continuous research.

Only if his product sells well and for more than its cost; only after government has preempted its half; only after depreciation; only after an adequate surplus has been set aside and an adequate amount allocated to research and reinvestment in new plants and equipment; only then can our "hazard" facing entrepreneur "hope" for a profit.

Maybe the question should be: "Why would anyone — *if there were no hope for a profit* — 'hazard' his lifetime savings or borrow capital; buy or lease land; buy, rent or erect a building; pay for raw materials; hire employees; train a sales force; advertise; insure; set up a depreciation fund; build up a surplus; invest in research — 'hoping' for earnings of which he knows in advance that the government will pocket one-half? Why not play it safe, let his nest-egg rest in peace in a government-insured bank account, go to work for some other dumb cluck, and let *him* risk losing *his* shirt?"

The simple truth is that if there were no "hope" for business profits, there would be no business. If there were no businesses, there would be no jobs. And if there were no jobs and no businesses, government would have no dollars to devote to social or to any other purposes.

It's elementary, but we all need to remember that, of itself, government has no money to devote to any purpose. Government has only what it takes away from *some* and theoretically feeds back to *others*. But in the collection and distribution process, inevitably the *receivers* get less than the *donors* give up. Governments can grow fat and bureaucratic off the difference.

So let's repeat. Profit is not a four-letter word. Profit is not a dirty word. Profit is not just a word.

Profits are precisely the essential catalyst without which the American economy just would not run. The vitalizing fuel which gives to us individuals, fortunate enough to live under a profit system, a standard of living which is the envy of the world.

But maybe profits are too big. Or maybe we all need to *know* just how big business profits really are!...

HOW BIG ARE PROFITS?

The Department of Commerce says that, for the year 1973, American business paid a *total* income tax bill of $56 billion. And that for the same year dividends to stockholders paid by *all* business added up to $28 billion.

So there you have it! *Two for one!* On the actual government record for 1973, and nationwide, American business devoted *$2* to "social purposes" from *pre-tax* earnings alone, vis-a-vis each *$1* paid stockholders in dividends from *after-tax* profits. But that is just *two-thirds* of the story.

You see, out of that $28 billion of dividends, stockholders still had to pay Uncle Sam no less than 23 per cent, or $6.4 billion in individual income taxes. Which, added to the $56 billion already preempted by government, made a total of $62.4 billion devoted to "social purposes." That left $21.6 billion in stockholders' pockets. So for *all* American business the actual ratio of business earnings devoted to "social purposes" in 1973, compared to dividends to stockohlders, was *$62.4* billion to *$21.6* billion. *That's $2.90 to $1.*

But even a ratio of *$2.90* devoted to "social purposes" for each *$1* paid stockholders doesn't tell *all* the story.

Business knows that it cannot thrive in an unhealthy economic milieu. So businesses — meaning sole proprietors, partnerships, corporations and individual businessmen — dig into their profits to share in "voluntarism" — that creature of American tradition which dates back to the Pilgrim Fathers. "Giving U.S.A." says that in 1973 voluntarism devoted $24.25 billion to philanthropy — to "social purposes."

It may be impossible to determine the exact dollar amount that business contributes to that $24.25 billion. Even so, business' share in that philanthropic purse cannot be ignored. Business abets an endless variety of educational, cultural, religious, research and welfare institutions which "strive to reach the hearts and minds of men and the physical well-being of mankind, and to give society its strength and quality."

As an example, business plays a part in the annual fund-raising drives of some 2,000 United Way organizations, providing almost a third of the money and much of the manpower. And the "gifts-in-kind" — "grants-in-aid" — equipment, products, loaned executives, etc., provided these and other such groups by business may be many times its dollar donations. "Giving U.S.A." lists 21 "Volunteer Strength Agencies," *national* in scope, to many if not most of which business lends assistance. Not to mention numberless local, social-purpose projects.

To such community-service activities must be added the philanthropy of socially oriented foundations created by American business, by businessmen who have prospered in business, and by their families.

A brochure published by the Amherst Wilder Foundation of St. Paul, Minn., for example, says it was established "to aid, assist and provide relief and charity for the worthy sick, aged and otherwise needy people." This relatively small foundation, with assets of about $31 million, valued at cost, devotes about $5.7 million a year to its stated purposes.

According to the Foundation Center, there are between 25,000 and 30,000 foundations operating in the United States. The Center is currently trying to determine which of about 2,500 foundations having assets of $1 million or more were established solely by business

corporations. Nineteen of the Dow Jones companies —
one short of two-thirds — have such foundations. A
partial list of business-family foundations devoted to
philanthropy, could be impressive. It still would not
give us the answer we seek. The extent of business
after-tax contributions to community problems could
well be the subject of a thorough-going study.

Let's make a truly conservative guesstimate.
Assume that business accounted for only 10 per cent of
that $24.25 billion of American voluntarism in 1973. So
add $2.4 billion of voluntarism'' contributions to the
$62.4 billion that government had already extracted
from business' pre-tax earnings, and from stockholders' dividends. That makes $64.8 billion devoted to
''social purposes.'' Let the $21.6 billion left for stock-
holders to spend stand — though surely they too
devoted some part of their after-tax dividend income to
voluntarism. Now we have a ratio of $64.8 billion to
$21.6 billion. *That's $3 for ''social purposes'' to each $1
for stockholders.* And until some statistical genius
comes up with a definite measure of business' share in
voluntarism, let's settle for a *minimum* overall ratio of
$3 for ''social purposes'' to $1 for stockholders'
dividends. Then — in totals for 1973 — *of $126.3
billion* of business earnings, all potential profit:

• *$62.4 billion* or 49 per cent was devoted to ''social
purposes.''

• *$42.3 billion* or 34 per cent was fed to the goose
that laid the golden eggs — hopefully, to maintain or
improve her productivity.

• *$21.6 billion* or 17 per cent — *less than one-fifth* —
was left for stockholders to spend.

• Or to reinvest in business, there again to devote *$3*
to ''social purposes'' and leave *$1* for stockholders to
spend.

The facts and figures used so far are from impec-
cable sources, leaving no room for question or doubt.
Except, indeed, for our guesstimate of business' share
in voluntarism which raised the social-purpose-stock-
holder ratio by all of 10 cents: from $2.90 to $3....

Peg the figure whenever you please. Whether it's as

little as $3 for $1, or as much as $5 for $1, or at some point in between; whether at the rate of 51 per cent or at 83 per cent or whatever; plainly *business devotes somewhere between one-half and four-fifths of its earnings to "social purposes."* And in any case stockholders keep less than one-fifth!

It's time to become factually informed. With information comes understanding. Public opinion can be polluted just as our air, our lakes and our rivers. Business is already spending a good part of its profits today to clean up other kinds of pollution. Maybe it must spend still more of its profits to anti-pollute public opinion.

"Why shouldn't business devote its profits to 'social purposes' "?

The answer is that it does — devoting between a minimum of *one-half* and as much as *four-fifths* of its over-all earnings to "social purposes."

MAJOR OIL COMPANIES SHOULD BE BROKEN UP

Birch Bayh

Birch Bayh is a liberal Democratic senator from Indiana. With Senator Philip Hart of Michigan, he has co-sponsored a bill to break up the large oil companies.

As you read try to answer the following questions:

1. What does Senator Bayh say vertical divestiture will not do?
2. Why does he claim divestiture is needed?
3. What examples does he give of concentration and monopoly in the oil industry?
4. What do the terms *vertical integration* and *divestiture* mean?

Birch Bayh, ''Should Major Oil Companies Be Broken Up? Yes!'' **The Christian Science Monitor**, June 11, 1976. Reprinted by permission from **The Christian Science Monitor** © 1976 The Christian Science Publishing Society. All rights reserved.

Having taken the lead, along with Senator Philip Hart of Michigan, in the Senate effort to require vertical divestiture in the oil industry, I must confess a bit of disappointment with the tactics of some who oppose our legislation. Certainly we expect no less than a thoroughgoing defense of its position by the oil industry. And Frank Ikard has testified before the Senate Antitrust and Monopoly Subcommittee with the kind of spirited and reasoned defense of the industry's structure that contributes to a constructive debate.

But certain of the oil industry's spokesmen have unfairly and incorrectly posed questions and raised issues that serve more to confuse than to enlighten. For this reason, it may make sense to briefly explain what divestiture will NOT do, before explaining why divestiture is in the public interest.

Vertical divestiture of the oil industry will NOT mean any reduction in the amount of gasoline, home heating oil, and other petroleum products available to consumers and industry. The profit motive or the exploration and production of oil will not be diminished by divestiture. Indeed, divestiture may well mean increased production, as some producers will lose the current incentive to hold down production in order to sustain higher prices at the retail end of their integrated operations.

Vertical divestiture of the oil industry will NOT mean increased government involvement in the industry. Quite the opposite. With the exception of public utilities, the oil industry is now the most closely regulated of all U.S. industries. Divestiture should open the door for the relaxation of such regulation by creating an atmosphere in which free enterprise can thrive. As long as a handful of companies maintain their tight control over all sectors of the industry there will continue to be the need for close government supervision and demands by some for a government takeover of the industry. As one who opposes a government takeover and who favors a truly free market, I am convinced that divestiture is necessary.

Vertical divestiture will NOT increase the power of the OPEC nations. Indeed vertical divestiture will help diminish the power of OPEC by ending the present situation in which the companies' downstream operations (refining and marketing) are dependent on the close relationship between the companies' producing arms and the OPEC nations.

Vertical divestiture will NOT hurt the position of oil company shareholders and employees. Shareholders will be justly compensated, either in cash or with new stock issues, for divested assets. There will not be any erosion of the pension rights of employees, whose rights are fully protected under existing law.

Vertical divestiture is NOT punitive; it is NOT designed to make the oil companies the innocent victims of our energy problem.

It is in the need to bring competition to this most basic of all industries, that the need for divestiture can best be understood.

Competition is absent from a large part of the oil industry because of a unique combination of vertical integration and intense concentration. To attempt to divert attention from the convergence of integration and concentration, the industry often cites statistics showing that other industries are more concentrated. And this is true. But none of those more concentrated industries controls so basic a commodity as oil, and none of those industries has comparable vertical integration.

The degree to which a small number of companies control oil from the time a drill bit enters the ground to start a new well until the time the gasoline refined from the oil in that well is pumped into the consumer's gasoline tank is remarkable. The 18 companies affected by Petroleum Industry Competition Act, as reported favorably by the Antitrust and Monopoly Subcommittee, control aproximately 75 percent of U.S. oil production, refining, and marketing and 90 percent of pipeline capacity.

This unique combination of integration and concentration has enabled a relatively small number of companies to administer prices, thwarting the operation of a free market in crude oil and refined products. To understand the economic consequences of the oil industry's structure, consider these examples:

1. Just a year ago U.S. refineries were operating at

about 85 percent of capacity despite an ample supply of crude oil. The reduced refinery runs created the threat of a gasoline shortage and enabled the oil companies to post and to sustain the maximum allowable increase in gasoline prices just prior to the July 4 peak driving period. The careful balancing of production, transportation, and refining necessary to succeed in such a gambit is dependent on vertical integration.

2. While oil producers in OPEC nations must obviously maintain a close association with the host countries, those ties have been intensified by the need of the same companies for an adequate supply of crude oil for their refineries and marketing outlets. Were the refineries independent of the production companies they would have an incentive, now lacking, to attempt to undermine the strength of OPEC through long-term contracts with individual countries.

3. An extensive staff study done for the Antitrust and Monopoly Subcommittee provided solid evidence that a number of major oil companies are not producing oil as efficiently as possible on federal off-shore leases in the Gulf of Mexico. One logical reason for the "holding down" of production would be the inability of an integrated company's refineries to fully utilize maximum efficient production.

4. Vertical integration has enabled the major oil companies to undercut the small, but highly competitive, independent sector of the oil industry.

The vertical divestiture legislation approved by the Anti-trust and Monopoly Subcommittee would separate the exploration and production operations of the 18 largest oil companies from their refining and marketing operations. In addition all significant crude oil and product pipelines would be ordered divested so that they can truly be common carriers providing equal access to all producers and refiners. Also, to prevent a further erosion of the position of dealer operated service stations further acquisition of retail outlets by integrated companies would be prohibited.

Clearly this is a far-reaching proposal. But the magnitude of the problem in the oil industry justifies such strong action; no step short of divestiture will provide an adequate response to the stranglehold the industry now has on consumers and industry.

MAJOR OIL COMPANIES SHOULD NOT BE BE BROKEN UP

by Frank N. Ikard

Frank Ikard has been President and Chief Executive Officer of the American Petroleum Institute since 1963.

Think of the following questions while you read:

1. What does Mr. Ikard claim is America's most important oil and energy problem?
2. Why does he claim charges of concentration and monopoly in the oil industry are false?
3. Why does he believe that the big American oil companies can bargain better with the oil producing nations of the Middle East (OPEC) than smaller companies?

Advocates of dismembering oil companies talk a great deal about "competition" and "concentration" but ignore the overriding question: What's in the best interests of consumers?

Rarely do they talk about how dismemberment would affect the supply of energy to consumers, or about the higher prices it would bring.

They focus instead on the side issues. This conjures up for me a vision of a couple of ordinary Americans returning to their home after a prolonged absence. Opening the door leading to the basement, they discover — to their utter horror — a pool or water two or three feet deep. There is a massive leak, and even as they are staring, water is pouring through a yawning hole in the foundation wall.

What to do? The first order of business ought to be stopping the leak and fixing up the foundation before the house starts to sag. It would surely be dangerous, at this time, to be sidetracked by less important matters.

For our nation, the "massive leak" is, of course, our increasing dependence on foreign oil. If the analogy seems overdrawn consider that our dependency on oil imports now amounts to more than 40 percent — more than before the Arab embargo of 1973-74. The Federal Energy Administration predicts a rise to 45 percent next year. It's highly likely that by 1980, we'll be importing 50 percent.

That massive and growing "leak" is also the core of our energy problem. No amount of proposals to break apart integrated companies will solve it. No amount of emotional rhetoric on the theme of "big is bad" will make it go away. We can't ignore it.

Not only is the proportion of imported oil increasing, the portion of imports coming from the Middle East countries that took part in the last embargo is increasing even faster. Canada is withdrawing completely as an oil supplier to the U.S. In the meantime, with an improving economy, we are stepping up our use of energy. The result is that imports from the Middle East members of OPEC have gone up from 18.3 percent of total demand in September, 1973 (just before the embargo) to 25 percent in October, 1975 — the latest figure available — and are going higher.

The import trend is of crucial importance because energy provides so much of the underpinning for our modern, industrialized society. There is no question, of course, but that our life-style could be a lot simpler. We waste energy to an appalling degree. But the goals and aspirations of most of us — for rewarding jobs, better schools, opportunities to travel and the like — are energy-related to an astonishing degree.

The 1973-74 embargo period highlighted those close ties. Some 500,000 jobs were lost simply because a portion of our energy was cut off. The effects of that event rippled through the whole economy, and are being felt even today.

One can only imagine the chaos that embargo might have caused — not only here in the U.S. but all around the world — without the huge transportation and marketing networks of the large integrated companies. An FEA study concluded that although the embargo was aimed at a particular set of countries, the international oil companies were able to even out the supply of crude oil to consuming nations, thus easing the embargo impact.

The integrated companies that are the targets of the congressional proposals comprise the most complex organizations in the world, in a highly complex industry. Their efficiency and expertise have been developed over many years, until today they constitute what amounts to a national asset. In the face of our increasingly vulnerability to another supply interruption, does it really make sense to scatter that expertise and efficiency?

Advocates of dismemberment — ignoring the central question of the impact of their proposals on consumers — claim the action is necessary because (1) there is excessive concentration in the industry — it needs "more competition"; (2) the OPEC cartel would thereby be pressured to lower oil prices.

The charge of "noncompetition" seems ludicrous when the average motorist can reel off the names of at least 14 or 15 companies that certainly seem competitive — else why would they put service stations across the street from each other? Even the congressional committee offering the latest dismemberment proposal — known as the Bayh-Hart bill — came up with 18 companies that would be affected.

The charge doesn't even make much sense to students of oligopoly, who point out that there are at least 25 other industries with higher "concentration ratios" than petroleum. So the charge has recently been reupholstered. It has been padded out with the

This is a monopoly.

Let's say you own this whole pie. And let's just say it's the only pie in the world. You can sell pie at whatever price you want, and people will have to pay it. You have a monopoly. That could be unfair.

But let's say you're a U. S. oil company. No matter which one you are, you only have a small piece of the pie. Not one American oil company accounts for more than 8½ percent of the oil produced in this country, and most produce a much smaller share. Now you don't have

thought that oil has such an unusual impact on the economy that its "concentration" shouldn't be compared with other industries.

But this latest argument also has its flaws. Surely, all our large, basic industries are interrelated. When the price of steel goes up, the cost of a drilling platform goes up. If automobiles use more gasoline, that affects demand for oil. There is only one respect in which the oil industry stands in isolation from others: it is the only

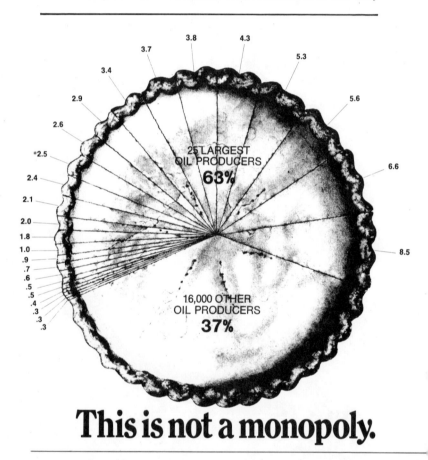

3.8 4.3
3.7
3.4   5.3
2.9
2.6   5.6
*2.5
2.4   6.6
2.1
2.0
1.8
1.0   8.5
.9
.7
.6
.5
.5
.4
.3
.3
.3

25 LARGEST
OIL PRODUCERS
63%

16,000 OTHER
OIL PRODUCERS
37%

This is not a monopoly.

a monopoly—you have competition. In fact, you have very stiff competition. That's fair.

By slicing up a monopoly, the government creates competition.

But by slicing up an already competitive situation, the government only creates . . . a mess.

This is a thought from a company with just a small piece of the pie.

*Our piece of the pie

industry under federal price and allocation controls.

Charges of "concentration" are meaningless without comparisons. The notion that dismemberment is somehow going to place restraints on the OPEC cartel is merely naive. It's based on the theory that separated, independent refining companies would be more aggressive bargainers for the OPEC oil than the major companies have been. There's simply no evidence at all for the contention, and certainly little reason to think that a large number of weaker companies will be better bargainers than the present major companies.

The principal fault with the proposals, however, is that they are simply diverting the country from the key problem: How can we reverse the growing dependence on imports? The structure and the size of the oil companies did not cause the energy problem, and no amount of rearranging of the companies will solve it.

If we are to deal effectively with the nation's long-term energy problem, we need to take the positive approach of shaping national energy policies that will lead us toward a higher degree of energy "independence." Even the advocates of dismemberment agree to this; but dismantling the companies with the proven ability to solve the problem seems a foolish way to start.

DISTINGUISHING PRIMARY FROM SECONDARY SOURCES

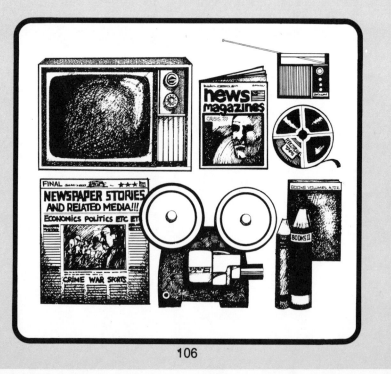

A rational person must always question his various sources of information. Scholars, for example, usually distinguish between **primary sources** (eyewitness accounts) and **secondary sources** (writings based on primary or eyewitness accounts, or other secondary sources). Most textbooks are examples of secondary sources. A diary written by a Civil War veteran, about the Civil War, is one example of a primary source. In order to be a critical reader one must be able to recognize primary sources. This, however, is not enough. Eyewitness accounts do not always provide accurate descriptions. Historians may find ten different eyewitness accounts that interpret an event differently. They must then decide which of these accounts provide the most objective and accurate interpretations. Also remember that primary sources are not always better than secondary sources. Frequently secondary sources will prove accurate, while primary sources can be unreliable.

Test your skill in evaluating sources by participating in the following exercise. Pretend you are living 2000 years in the future. Your teacher tells you to write an essay about the economic situation in America between 1960 and 1980. First, consider carefully each of the following sources and locate the **primary** (eyewitness) accounts. Second, rank **all** sources by assigning the number (1) to the source you think might be the most objective and accurate. Assign the number (2) to the next most accurate and so on until the ranking is finished. See if you can find any secondary sources that might be better than a primary source.

Since most sources cited below are fictitious, you cannot read and judge their accuracy. You will, however, recognize some of the people mentioned. You must guess about how their frame of reference and political views might influence perceptions of economics. The activity is designed to help you begin exploring the kind of source analysis needed for intelligent and rational thinking about social issues. Assume that all of the following sources deal with the broad issue of economics in America. Discuss and compare your source evaluations with other class members.

_____ a. A televised interview in 1978 of Jimmy Carter

_____ b. A magazine article written in 1991 by a leading American liberal economist

_____ c. A radio interview in 1993 of a leading American conservative economist

_____ d. A newspaper editorial written in 1979 by a leading Canadian economist who specializes in the study of economics in America

_____ e. A book written in 1977 by a U.S. Senator critical of large corporations

_____ f. A Senate speech made in 1975 by a U.S. Senator who believed that reducing corporate taxes was the best way to stimulate the economy

_____ g. An essay written in 1978 by a leading American sociologist

_____ h. A speech made in 1979 by a president of a large corporation

_____ i. A taped interview in 1965 of an English economist who specializes in the study of economics in America

_____ j. A book written in 1990 by a leading Japanese economist who specializes in the study of economics in America

CHAPTER 4

TAX REFORM

TAX LOOPHOLES FAVOR THE POOR

Roger A. Freeman

Roger A. Freeman is a Senior Fellow Emeritus at Stanford University.

As you read try to answer the following questions:

1. What people does the author say benefit from untaxed income?
2. Why does he say it is difficult to close tax loopholes?
3. How does he define the ''conspiracy theory of tax law?''
4. What changes in the tax laws does Mr. Freeman suggest?
5. How do you interpret the cartoon in this reading?

Roger A. Freeman, ''Tax Loopholes,'' **Vital Speeches**, December 1, 1975, pp. 102-08. Reprinted with permission from **Vital Speeches Of The Day**.

For close to twenty years so-called loopholes in the federal income tax have been the subject of sharp and noisy public controversy....

It is thus not surprising that the Congress took repeated action to close loopholes in the income tax — in 1969, 1971, and again in 1975. What may be surprising is the fact that every time Congress enacted a tax reform bill, the amount of untaxed income was larger afterwards than it had been before and the percentage of total personal income exempted from the federal income tax as well as the number of Americans paying no income tax had substantially increased. In other words, whenever Congress tightened or closed some loopholes — or acted as if it had — it always opened or widened others more extensively. This is not only an expression of the old maxim — in politics and elsewhere — that it is more blessed to give than to receive. It strongly suggests that the real aim of the "close the loopholes" drive is not so much to subject more taxfree personal income to the tax as to shift the burden of taxation from some economic groups to others — to tax some more lightly and others more heavily. To be specific, the real goal and purpose of the campaign to close loopholes is to redistribute income from some less favored groups — presumably from groups with less voting power — to some with more votes and therefore greater political appeal to office holders and office seekers.

The amounts we are talking about here are not exactly chicken feed. All personal income in the United States totalled $945 billion in 1972 (according to the national income and products accounts) of which only $445 billion showed up as taxable on federal income tax return. In other words, $500 billion — or 53 percent of all personal income — went tax free in 1972, up from $363 billion or 48 percent in 1969. Counting offsetting items — amounts which are taxed although they are not personal income under prevailing economic definitions — untaxed income totalled $563 billion in 1972, up from $414 billion in 1969.

TAX REFORM

That increase in taxfree income is easily explained

by the fact that several "tax reform" measures went into effect between 1969 and 1972, undertaken to close loopholes and to capture formerly exempt income. The main factor was the Tax Reform Act of 1969, the most extensive, intricate and confusing amendment to the Internal Revenue Code ever enacted which has since become more affectionately known as the Lawyers and Accountants Full Employment Act of 1969. About $70 billion in personal income escaped federal income taxation in 1972 as a direct consequence of the Tax Reform Act of 1969.

You are probably acquainted with complaints that the property tax and the sales tax permit many exemptions which have eroded the tax base and thereby not only cut the revenues of schools, cities and states but also given advantages to certain favored groups of taxpayers over others. But exemptions in the property and sales taxes equal only between one-fourth and one-third of their respective tax bases. In the federal income tax they total more than half the base — and it has become the leakiest tax known.

Yet the income tax is by far the most important revenue producer in our fiscal system. Individual and corporate income taxes accounted for 52 percent of all revenues in the federal Unified Budget. Following the classification of the Bureau of the Census, which places social insurance contributions in a different category — income taxes provide regularly 80 percent to 85 percent of all federal tax revenues. While the United States imposed a personal income tax later than most other industrial nations — in 1913, after the adoption of the XVI Amendment to the U.S. Constitution — it now leans more heavily on income taxes — graduate personal income tax and corporate profits tax — than any other major country. Other industrial countries use a general consumption tax as a major producer of revenue for their national government. The United States is the only country not to do so.

Yet it has restricted the personal income tax base to less than half of the personal income. If all exclusions, exemptions, deductions and credits were repealed and *all* personal income were subjected to the tax, the tax rates could be halved — from the present 14 percent to 70 percent range to a 7 percent to 35 percent range. Alternatively, a flat 10 percent tax on *all* personal income would yield about as much revenue as the present rate scale on half the income. Some would favor such a system, although many lawyers and accountants, not to mention members of the staff of the Internal Revenue Service, would lose their jobs. But there is not a chance in a million that such a plan could ever be adopted. The simple facts of political arithmetic — of counting where the votes are — rule it out.

The tax reform movement, the drive "to close the loopholes" does not aim to tax all income, or more income than is presently taxed, but to tax some types of income more heavily so that either the government can spend more than it does now or that additional tax relief be granted to certain favored groups....

The plain fact is that most of the $563 billion in untaxed income is in the middle and lower income brackets, is broadly distributed through all sections of the American public with only a tiny percentage accruing to high-income persons. The truth is that most high income persons pay very high income taxes.

THE BIG LOOPHOLES

What then are the big "loopholes," the provisions which account for most of the $563 billion of untaxed income in 1972? By far the largest loophole is personal exemptions — at $750 a head — which total $155 billion. Many feel that $750 is not enough, that it costs more to support a child. That may well be true. But then, why should the U.S. Government pay a tax bonus for every child at a time when we are trying to reduce population growth and reach ZPG? Should there not rather be a penalty than a premium?

Taxfree income from social benefits — social security, unemployment compensation, public assistance, veterans benefits, employer contributions to pension and welfare funds and other transfer payments account for another $93 billion. Those remedial provisions redound largely to the benefit of low-income and low-to-middle-income persons. Little of it goes to wealthy families.

The other big item is itemized deductions — for state and local taxes, interest paid, charitable dona-

113

tions, medical expenses, casualty losses, etc. They totalled in 1972 $97 billion. But the fact is that those itemized deductions equalled 55 percent of reported income on returns itemizing deductions in the adjusted gross income (AGI) bracket under $5000, 20 percent in the $15,000 to $25,000 income bracket, and 22 percent in the income class from $100,000 on up. In other words, itemized deductions free a much larger share of the income from taxation in the low brackets than in the high. More importantly, most persons in the lower income brackets use the standard deduction instead of itemizing. Under the liberalized provisions of the Tax Reform Act of 1969, standard deductions more than tripled between 1969 and 1972 — from $22 billion to $70 billion — while income increased only 26 percent and itemized deductions 21 percent. This simplified the preparation of an additional 10 million returns. It also freed huge amounts of income from taxation for no other justifiable reason. While civilian employment expanded 5 percent between 1969 and 1972, the number of taxable income tax returns *declined* 5 percent, the number of *nontaxable* returns increased 38 percent, jumping from 12 million returns to 17 million. Of the $70 billion standard deductions in 1972 only $24 billion were percentage standard deudctions (15 percent up to $2000) $46 billion were for low income allowances.

Of the $301 billion difference between adjusted gross income (AGI) and taxable income (TI) on 1972 income tax returns $127 billion were in brackets from $50,000 income on up. In other words, 58 percent of all AGI of persons under $10,000 were taxfree, only 24 percent of the AGI of persons in the $50,000 and up brackets were.

That still leaves the possibility open that many rich people pay little or no income taxes. I'll discuss that in detail a little later. But the fact stands out that most of the untaxed income accrues to low to middle income recipients and not to wealthy persons.

The conspiracy theory of tax law — that loopholes are the result of sinister machinations of lobbyists for moneyed interests who either bribed lawmakers or pulled the wool over the eyes of unsuspecting congressmen and the public — won't stand up under examination....

THE RICH

Recipients of .an AGI between $7000 and below $20,000 accounted in 1972 for 57 percent of the reported income and paid 49 percent of the tax. So, clearly they were not overburdened relative to the rest of the population. The real shift is between the groups at the top and at the bottom of the scale: those under $7000 income received 16 percent of AGI and paid 6.5 percent of the tax; those at $20,000 and up received 27 percent of AGI and paid 44 percent of the tax. In rough terms, persons at the $20,000 and up level got about one-fourth of all income and paid nearly one-half of the income tax. Surely they are not in a "favored" position.

For 1972, 22,929 individual income tax returns were filed with an AGI of $200,000 or more; 22,821 of those returns or 99.5 percent were taxable. They reported an average AGI of $414,640, an average taxable income of $302,015 on which they paid a tax of $177,640, or an average rate of 59 percent. There were 108 returns (= 0.5 percent) with an adjusted gross income of $200,000 or more which reported no taxable income, because of losses, deductions etc. and paid no tax.

There were 1030 returns with an AGI of $1 million or more of which 1024 (= 99.4 percent) were taxable. Each individual involved paid on the average $1,019,577 in income tax, equal to 46 percent of his AGI and 65 percent of his taxable income.

What this means is that well over 99 percent of all high-income returns for 1972 paid high income taxes. Between 0.5 percent and 0.6 percent of the earners of a high *gross* income reported no taxable *net* income because losses, deductions, credits, or other offsetting items exceeded their gross income. Obviously it is only under very unusual circumstances that recipients of a high *gross* income have no taxable *net* income....

There were altogether 16.7 million individual income tax returns in 1972 which reported no taxable income — 21.5 percent of all 77.6 million returns. Ninety-two percent of the nontaxable returns were in the under $5000 AGI bracket. At $10,000 and above AGI only 0.4 percent of the returns were not taxable. In summary, the charges that loopholes enable many rich people to escape income taxation while being unavailable to low-income persons is a perversion of truth, political propaganda intended to stir up jealousy, envy, hatred and class warfare. The real goal of such claims is to redistribute income more drastically than is already done, from those who earn it to those who yearn it...

IN CONCLUSION:

In its allocation of mitigative features — or "loop-holes" if you please — the federal income tax shows the same bias which characterizes the entire American tax structure: in favor of consumption and against capital formation and investment, in favor of the low (or no) producer and against the high producer and earner.

That is politically understandable. Four out of every five personal income tax returns in 1972 reported an AGI under $15,000 and 95 percent were under $25,000. On the other hand, only 3 percent of all returns showed AGI of $30,000 or more and a mere 0.8 percent of $50,000 or over. With whom is the vote hungry member of Congress or candidate going to place his bet — and vote: with the 51 percent who report an income under $8000 or with the 0.8 percent with an income of $50,000 or more?

But the American people are paying a high price for this bias — in a much lower rate of investment than is enjoyed by other industrial countries, in a smaller rate of economic growth, and in higher unemployment.

Even more ominous is the creation of a growing mass of people who clamor for ever greater benefits from the government to whose support they do not have to contribute. The growing irresponsibility of voting — of representation without taxation — poses a grave threat to the preservation of free government in the United States. History issues a stern warning which we can neglect at our dire peril.

TAX LOOPHOLES FAVOR THE RICH

Walter S. Mondale

Walter F. Mondale is a Democratic Senator from Minnesota. He is a leading Senate liberal and has been active in support of tax reform.

Think of the following questions while you read:

1. What evidence does Senator Mondale give to support his contention that most tax breaks go to the rich?
2. What changes does he propose in the tax laws?
3. How does the cartoon in this reading support what the author is saying?

Senator Walter F. Mondale, **Congressional Record**, June 2, 1975.

A Treasury study prepared at my request shows that the benefits from most "tax expenditures" — preferential tax provisions intended to encourage or reward specific activities — are concentrated heavily on taxpayers with the highest incomes.

Of the $58 billion in fiscal year 1974 tax expenditures, over 23 percent went to individuals with incomes of over $50,000, who make up only 1.2 percent of all taxpayers.

The 160,000 taxpayers with incomes of $100,000 or more received an average of $45,662 each in tax relief from the 57 tax expenditures on the Treasury list, while the 9.9 million taxpayers earning between $15,000 and $20,000 saved an average of only $901 apiece, and those from $10,000 to $15,000 saved only $556 each.

Tax expenditures are defined by the new Congressional Budget Act as the revenue losses attributable to Federal tax provisions —

> which allow a special exclusion, exemption or deduction from gross income or which provide a special credit, a preferential rate of tax, or a deferral of tax liability.

The Senate Budget Committee, on which I serve, is required by the new law:

> To request and evaluate continuing studies of tax expenditures, to devise methods of coordinating tax expenditures, policies and programs with direct budget outlays, and to report the results of such studies to the Senate on a recurring basis.

The 57 tax expenditures on the Treasury list include the special tax treatment of capital gains, $6.7 billion; the tax exemption for state and local bond interest, $1.1 billion; excess depreciation deductions, $700 million; the investment tax credit, $880 million; deductions for home mortgage interest, $4.9 billion; property taxes, $4.1 billion; and medical expenses, $2.1 billion; and a variety of other provisions.

Many of the larger expenditures are very heavily concentrated in the higher income brackets. Over 88 percent of the $1.1 billion in tax relief going to individuals from tax-exempt State and local bonds goes to people with incomes over $50,000.

Over 62 percent of the $6.7 billion tax expenditure from the special tax treatment of capital gains goes to the 1.2 percent of taxpayers with incomes over $50,000, and over 47 percent goes to those with incomes over $100,000.

Reprinted with permission from **The Daily World**.

THE TAX EXPENDITURE CONCEPT

There is a good deal of misunderstanding about the concept of tax expenditures.

The concept is based on the assumption that the main purpose of an income tax system is simply to raise revenue, and that all taxpayers and all forms of income should, as nearly as possible, be treated alike. There are, of course, broad exceptions to this rule, such as the progressive rate structure and the provisions which take into account differing family sizes, but these are considered part of the basic structure of our income tax system.

However, when the Government seeks to use the tax system for other, more limited, purposes — to encourage oil drilling, exports, business investment, home building, and so forth — by giving preferential tax treatment to those who engage in those activities, it is in effect subsidizing them with money that must be made up by higher tax collections from others.

The practical effect is the same as if the Government took a portion of its tax revenues and made a direct grant to those who engage in the activities the Government wants to encourage or reward.

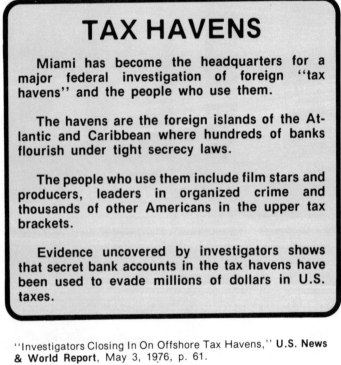

TAX HAVENS

Miami has become the headquarters for a major federal investigation of foreign "tax havens" and the people who use them.

The havens are the foreign islands of the Atlantic and Caribbean where hundreds of banks flourish under tight secrecy laws.

The people who use them include film stars and producers, leaders in organized crime and thousands of other Americans in the upper tax brackets.

Evidence uncovered by investigators shows that secret bank accounts in the tax havens have been used to evade millions of dollars in U.S. taxes.

"Investigators Closing In On Offshore Tax Havens," **U.S. News & World Report**, May 3, 1976, p. 61.

But instead of collecting the money from all taxpayers and granting it back to some taxpayers, it allows the favored taxpayers to keep the money and make it up by collecting more from everyone else.

These tax expenditures are thus a form of Government spending or subsidy, and they should be evaluated on the same basis as other forms of Government spending.

Calling these special tax provisions expenditures does not make them either good or bad. It is meant to be a neutral term, and it is intended only to require us to begin looking at these tax subsidies in the same way we look at other Federal spending programs. Their practical effect is the same, and they should be judged by the same standards.

ESCAPING TAXES

A total of 244 Americans with adjusted gross incomes of $200,000 or more paid no income tax in 1974, the Internal Revenue Service [IRS] said Wednesday, compared with 164 who paid no tax in 1973.

"IRS Says 244 Had Gross Income of $200,000 in 1974, but Paid no Tax," **Minneapolis Tribune**, May 6, 1976, p. 7A.

Many tax expenditures serve a legitimate purpose and they should be continued. Others need to be examined to see whether they can be restructured so that their benefits are distributed more broadly and equitably. In still other cases, a direct expenditure, loan or guarantee program might work better than a tax expenditure, and we should consider substituting one for the other. And finally, some tax expenditures serve no defensible purpose at all, and should be abolished.

The new budget process will enable the Congress to review and analyze these tax expenditures in the same way we look at other Federal spending programs, so that we can make certain they are serving the purposes for which they were intended efficiently and at the lowest possible cost.

CONCENTRATION IN HIGHER BRACKETS

The concentration of tax expenditure benefits in the higher income brackets is one of the important reasons that provisions must be examined with great care. If the Federal Government is, in effect, going to be spending money to support or reward certain activities, we must determine whether it makes sense to do so under a system which provides the highest benefits to those with the highest incomes.

One reason why most tax expenditures provide more relief to those with higher incomes, is that they exclude or exempt from taxation income which would otherwise be taxed at a taxpayer's highest marginal rate. As a result, the tax benefit from a provision increases as a taxpayer's highest marginal tax bracket increases. For a taxpayer in the lowest, 14-percent bracket — making around $5,000 a year — each $100 deduction, exclusion or exemption is worth only $14 in reduced taxes. But for someone in the highest, 70-percent bracket — making over $200,000 a year — each $100 deduction, exclusion or exemption is worth $70 in reduced taxes.

This problem could be avoided by changing deductions or exemptions into credits. Unlike a deduction, a credit is subtracted directly from the tax otherwise due, so it is worth the same amount in tax savings to all taxpayers, no matter what marginal tax bracket they are in. A $100 credit would save everyone $100 in taxes, rather than saving the rich $70 and the poor $14.

I have proposed, for example, that taxpayers be given the choice of taking a $200 credit for themselves and each dependent, instead of the present $750 personal exemption. This $200 optional credit would be worth more in tax savings than the $750 exemption to almost all families earning $20,000 or less.

The Senate approved this $200 optional credit earlier this year as part of the Tax Reduction Act, but it was dropped in conference and replaced by a $30 credit which may be taken in addition to the $750 exemption.

The use of a credit rather than a deduction could well be extended to other areas, such as the provisions dealing with home mortgage interest and property taxes. If properly structured, the credit could result in greater tax savings than the present deductions for the great majority of taxpayers.

READING 19

CORPORATE TAXES SHOULD BE SLASHED

Jack Kemp

Congressman Jack Kemp is a Republican from New York's 38th district in the U.S. House of Representatives since 1970. He is currently a member of the House Appropriations Committee and the subcommittees on Defense and the District of Columbia.

Consider the following questions while reading:

1. According to the author, what do high corporate taxes do to our economy?
2. How does he say cutting corporate taxes would bolster the economy?
3. Does the cartoon in this reading support any of the author's ideas?

Jack Kemp, **Congressional Record**, April 8, 1975.

Taxes come ultimately from the people. They pay some taxes directly: Individual income taxes, sales taxes, gasoline and fuel taxes, gift and estate taxes. They pay others indirectly through higher prices they pay for goods and services they purchase: Corporate income taxes, real estate and sales taxes paid by businesses, and so forth. The point is: The people pay all the taxes.

WHAT HIGH CORPORATION TAXES DO TO OUR ECONOMY

High corporate tax burdens — American corporations today pay almost a 50-percent tax on their incomes — mean a number of things.

First. They must pass along those taxes to the consumers in the form of higher prices. Almost all corporate income comes from sales. The only way to recover the costs of taxes is through what they charge for goods and services. If corporate taxes were reduced, prices all of us pay could be reduced.

Second. They have less net dollars to spend for inventory replacement, replacement of equipment, purchase of new equipment, and expansion of plant facilities. That means a loss of jobs in two ways. It means the construction trades which build the plants will not be building them, so unemployment in the construction trades goes up or does not go down. It also means the loss of jobs in the company that wanted to replace its equipment or the deferral of plans to create new jobs because additional, new equipment and facilities have not been bought or built.

Third. The companies paying these high corporate taxes do not have sufficient funds to pay higher salaries to their employees or to increase the share paid by the company to retirement and pension funds or to increase other fringe benefits. This means less income to the work force.

Fourth. The companies are left with less funds from which to pay dividends to those who own shares of stock in the companies — and that is millions of people — little people, middle-class people, working men and women, retired people, widows — who depend upon dividends to maintain their standards of living.

WHY ADEQUATE CAPITAL IS ESSENTIAL TO ASSURE PROSPERITY

This last effect of high corporate taxes is one of crucial importance to the long-term growth of the American economy and the maintenance of the prosperity which has been associated with our free enterprise system — the greatest, most productive economic system known in man's history — a system which has been a mainstay of the reasons and emotions which make us proud of America and its history.

I speak, of course, of the necessity of having sufficient investment capital to assure the continued growth of the economy. We do not now have sufficient investment capital, and high tax burdens placed on industry and business are one of its principal causes....

TAXING EFFICIENCY

Corporate taxes are devised in such a way that the efficient producer is punished. His industrial expansion is restricted, his capital formation is prevented, and the competitiveness of American industry in international trade is damaged. Thus, the American tax system receives no payment at all from millions who are unproductive, while stifling the initiative of those who are productive by taxing away that portion of income which would be re-invested — creating new jobs and helping the economy to expand.

Allan C. Brownfeld, "Some Tax Reforms That Would Help," **Human Events**, November 22, 1975, p. 926-27.

HOW CUTTING CORPORATE TAXES WOULD BOLSTER THE ECONOMY, 1975-85

Cutting corporate taxes is the quickest — and the most enduring — way to put people back to work and create new jobs....

Corporations face some hard facts today. So, too, do the people who depend upon them for jobs and for goods and services, and that means all of us. What are some of those hard facts?

A tabulation of growth rates by the Organization for Economic Cooperation and Development of 20 advanced economies for 1960-70 put the United States in 18th place — third from the bottom.

We anticipate a capital shortfall of $1.5 trillion — that is 1,500 times $1 billion — over the next 10 years in what it will take to assure continued growth in our prosperity — even to stay at the standard of living at which we now find ourselves — to avoid sliding even further backward. This shortfall means we will be underinvesting $400 million each and every day for a full decade.

These startling figures are why I believe the highest priority of our economy should lie in the nurture and stimulation of capital formation — for corporations, for small businesses, for farmers — because everything the American people want and need grows out of that capital formation.

What could happen in this country if we do meet this challenge is so encouraging that every Member of Congress ought to be working every day to assure it. Assume that we meet this challenge and invest sufficient capital to sustain a 4.2-percent real growth rate.

America in 1985 would have:

First. A 43-percent decline in the number of people living in poverty — which means 10.6 million fewer poor people.

Second. A total of 17 million more jobs for Americans — the work force would grow from 86 million to 103 million people — up a full 20 percent.

Third. An increase in median family income of 59.2 percent, up from $12,051 in 1974 to $19,191 by 1985 — based on constant, not inflated, dollars — a growth in real income of nearly 60 percent.

And, *fourth*, 31.6 million more housing units — up

47 percent from 1970, leaving only 5 percent of total housing substandard — a 40-percent improvement over 1970.

These indices reflect substantial potential growth.

HOW CONGRESS SHOULD PROCEED TO ASSURE ECONOMIC GROWTH

Economic growth — and the recreation of jobs — can be best assured through inducements to capital formations.

We should provide sufficient inducements to assure a growing base of personal savings.

We should establish more realistic guidelines for depreciation allowances.

We should give better tax treatment for retained corporate earnings used for investment purposes.

We must ameliorate our relatively harsh treatment of capital gains compared with that of most other countries.

We must stabilize our fiscal and monetary policies to prevent violent swings in the economy.

And, we should eliminate unnecessary controls — those outmoded regulations that unduly restrict the economic system and push prices up and production down.

THE PROPOSED JOBS FORMATION ACT

Measures have been introduced to accomplish these objectives.

On March 20, I introduced the proposed Fiscal Integrity Act of 1975, H.R. 5293 and H.R. 5294, with over 30 cosponsors. That bill would limit the growth of Government — and thereby bring substantial stability to our fiscal and monetary policies — by establishing a limit on the size of total Federal Government revenue. In no fiscal year in the future could the size of those revenues — measured in terms of total national income — exceed the percentage those revenues bear to such income in the fiscal year in which the bill were enacted. Government's revenue could grow, in dollar terms but it could not grow in relation to the peoples' total incomes. That is crucial to limit the size of Government in relation to the totality of our society. That bill would also require balanced budgets, thereby eliminating the deficit borrowing which robs the capital markets of the funds essential to growth in the private sector.

On March 13, I introduced what can be considered the first, rough draft of the second component of these measures: inducements to capital formation through changes in our tax laws. That bill, the proposed Jobs Formation Act, H.R. 4906, consists of sections which fall into three basic categories of tax reform conducive to capital formation: Income tax reforms relating to individuals, such reforms relating to corporations, and employee stockownership plan financing.

Specific tax reform measures proposed in the bill include an exclusion from gross income for certain qualified savings and investments up to $500 per year, or $1,000 for a joint return; granting a $1,000 exclusion from capital gains for each capital transaction; granting an extension of time for payment of estate taxes where the estate consists largely of small business interests; increasing the estate tax exemption for family farming operations to $200,000; amending the corporate normal tax rates, including provision for reduced taxes for small businesses; increasing the investment tax credit and making it permanent, an essential requisite for long-term business planning; increasing the corporate surtax exemption, allowing taxable year price level adjustment in property — indexing; increasing class life variances for purposes of depreciation — ADR's; providing for alternative amortization periods for pollution control facilities which do not add to productivity; and, expanding the scope of employee stockownership plan financing. In addition, there will be included — in the amended, ''clean'' version of the bill — an elimination of the present double taxation of common dividends — now taxed once at the corporate level and once at the individual level....

The potential losses to the Treasury will be important in our analysis as to final recommendations, but it is important to stress that we have already introduced a bill to require balanced budgets and have made calls for reductions in expenditures down to the level of income. Therefore, these losses to the Treasury, in our proposed policy and program, would not be inflationary, because expenditures, under the other component of the overall plan, would be held to the level of income.

A revised Jobs Formation Act will be introduced within the coming days. I welcome cosponsors of it.

This point — congressional support for such measures — is itself an important one. I find a growing number of Members who are more acutely aware of the pivotal role of capital formation and of the necessity of congressional action to foster that formation. Fewer than that number, however, are willing to be broadly identified with tax reforms which appear ''pro-business.''

This program...is no more pro-business than it is pro-labor. It simply is pro-jobs, and it is jobs which we need more than anything else in the economy today — jobs which do not depend upon taxes — as do public service jobs. I deplore the all too true point made by the **Wall Street Journal** that Congress may realize what the problem is but that it does not have the courage to correct it through inducements to capital formation...

When one considers that all taxes are paid by the people, and when one further considers that disincentives and outright discouragement of capital formation in our present laws must be changed to nurture the capital formation which we so badly need, this is the way in which we should proceed.

CORPORATE TAXES SHOULD BE INCREASED

Charles A. Vanik

Charles A. Vanik is a Democratic Congressman from Ohio. He has been a leading critic of tax breaks for large corporations and for rich people. He has carried out four annual corporate tax studies detailing the taxes paid by large corporations.

Bring the following questions to your reading:

1. How and when were large corporations able to escape paying any taxes? How many companies avoided taxes?
3. What changes in the tax laws does he suggest?

Charles A. Vanik, **Congressional Record**, October 7, 1975.

I have requested recognition today in order to present to the Congress and the public my 4th annual corporate tax study on America's leading corporations. These computations, for tax year 1974, were prepared by expert congressional accountants from information that is entirely public.

The study obtained tax data on 142 of the 164 companies that we undertook to examine. Twenty-two companies either lost money or did not report their tax data in a manner that allowed congressional accountants to compute effective tax rates.

I want to stress that the figures are approximate figures and may reflect tendencies by companies to overstate or understate their tax statistics. It would not be unfair, however, to say that if anything, these figures and the computed effective tax rates are very kind to the corporations. The appendix to the study includes a more detailed explanation of the limitations of the data used to compute approximate incomes and approximate effective tax rates.

ESCAPING TAXES

As I have found in each of the last three years, there are some companies that pay no federal income taxes at all or actually were able to receive refunds from the IRS through tax credits, carrybacks, or carryforwards. In 1974, there were eight companies in the study who were able to escape paying Federal corporate income taxes completely despite a total profit of $843,974,000.

Additionally, there were 18 companies who were able to pay an approximate effective U.S. income tax rate of 10 percent or less, or $270,430,000 in taxes on $5,322,683,000 in profits. We all should recall that the corporate income tax rate, with some exceptions, is a statutory 48 percent.

In the previous tax year, 1973, my study found that 10 corporations, with total profits of approximately $976,000,000 paid no taxes. Another 20 corporations, making $5,285,555,000 in profits, paid effective Federal income taxes at a rate less than 10 percent for a total of $226,894,000 in Federal income taxes.

Although fewer companies escaped paying Federal

131

income taxes in 1974 and their profits were also down a small amount, it is very clear that the corporate sector is continuing to reduce its proportionate contribution to the support of the Federal Government. Congress must deal with the issue of shrinking corporate taxation over the long term.

Mr. Speaker, I must also stress that these corporations were able to completely avoid paying Federal income taxes or keep them to an absolute minimum without breaking any laws. They have instead taken very effective advantage of the numerous "incentives" and business sector "stimulants" that have come to be an established part of the United States Tax Code. Although some "tax relief" is available to individual taxpayers in the form of personal deductions — and tax rebates and reductions from the Tax Reductions Act of 1975 — it is miniscule when compared to the opportunities that America's corporations have to reduce their taxes.

These corporations do pay, just as the individual taxpayer, other, non-income-related taxes. These other taxes can include sales taxes, excise taxes, state, city or local taxes, franchise taxes, taxes to foreign governments, et cetera. Although companies included in my previous tax studies have been quick to claim that measuring only Federal income taxes is unfair or misleading, we all should keep in mind that individuals also pay more than just simple Federal income taxes. As a Member of Congress, my legislative jurisdiction extends only to Federal taxes, and an examination of effective Federal income taxes is essential in assessing the Federal Tax Code and its effects.

The figures on 1974's corporate tax rates continue to show that for large corporations, the 48-percent corporate tax rate is usually fiction — corporations are able to avoid to a large extent the statutory corporate tax level. The average effective Federal income tax rate for all companies in the study was only 22.6 percent, not even half of the 48-percent corporate rate....

Despite this deplorable level of corporate nontax-payment, business lobbies and the administration are pushing hard for new and additional tax breaks in their drive to enhance capital formaton. But if U.S. corporations are already paying little or nothing in Federal income taxes, it makes no sense to give them tax relief in an effort to stimulate investment capital....

Utilities were able to reduce their already small 1973 tax rate by almost 4 percentage points, from 18 to 14.1 percent. Consequently, utilities stand to gain very little from the administration's tax relief proposals. With close to one-fourth of the utility industry already not paying Federal income taxes, tax relief is like carrying coals to Newcastle. Furthermore, the 1975 amendments to the tax code increasing the investment credit from 4 to 10 percent for utilities will substantially eliminate utilities from the rolls of Federal income taxpayers....

THE VANIK REPORT

The report, prepared by Rep. Charles Vanik [D., Ohio] and the staff of the Joint Committee on Internal Revenue Taxation, notes that in 1974 the average effective federal income tax rate for 110 concerns studied was only 22.6 per cent, less than half the official levy and down from 23.6 per cent in 1973.

For 1974, the report said, eight corporations with profits totaling $844 million paid no federal income tax at all. Another eighteen companies with $5.3 billion in profits paid at an effective rate of less than 10 per cent. At the 48 per cent rate, the twenty-six corporations would have owed $2.95 billion. As it was, they paid only $220 million in federal income taxes.

"The Vanik Report," **The Nation**, December 20, 1975, p. 644.

Although revenue from individual income taxes declined in 1974, corporate income tax revenue also went down, meaning that some area of noncorporate taxpayer must make up the difference. This is a point... that I want to stress. For every revenue dollar lost to incentives or tax stimulants or just plain tax loopholes, the American public reaches into their pocket for another dollar to replace it.

133

Capital formation advocates, for instance, have so far not made any mention of where they expect the billions needed for capital formation to come from — unless it is to come from some kind of negative income tax for needy corporations....

As in each of my previous corporate tax studies, the 1974 compilations reveal several important things.

First, by listing payment to foreign governments, the study reveals the pervasive involvement of America's giant corporations in overseas operations. The giant corporations are no longer U.S. corporations — they are worldwide organizations, possibly beyond the control or supervision of any single government or other public agency. Public policy decisions about the regulations of giant corporations must understand that many of these organizations are world empires, often with resources larger than the countries in which they operate.

The extent of foreign involvement can be seen by the fact that the 110 industrial corporations paid $13,923,027,000 to foreign governments and only $8,383,652 to the U.S. Treasury in corporate income taxes. Even the major U.S. banks are no longer really "American" — they paid $385,633,000,000 to foreign governments but only $174,279,000 to the United States in corporate income taxes.

CHANGING THE TAX CODE

The tax code should be altered to deemphasize large conglomerates in favor of smaller businesses which are currently unable to take effective advantage of the myriad of tax incentives. Encouraging small business will also have the indirect effect of promoting competition and discouraging monopolistic situations.

Second, oil companies continue to pay almost no Federal income taxes despite large profits. A committee print of the Joint Committee on Internal Revenue Taxation entitled, "Taxation of Foreign Source Income, Statistical Data," and issued September 30, 1975, indicated that no net U.S. tax on foreign source income was paid by the petroleum industry in 1974. While the oil companies' worldwide effective tax rates appear high, this is misleading, since oil companies are allowed to treat foreign oil royalties as a foreign "tax" and thus qualify for the foreign tax credit. It is particularly important that oil tax reform be considered given our domestic crude shortages and the need to develop a complete energy policy.

Third, banks continue to be a powerful and growing force in our country through their diversification into nontraditional bank investment, particularly leasing. The tendency for large banks to expand into multinational operations should be examined by the Congress.

Fourth, utilities continue to pay little if any Federal income taxes and thus plans by the administration to aid them through additional tax relief measures will have little effect. Since utilities are regulated monopolies and assured a fair rate of return through their governing public utility commissions, Federal subsidization through the tax code is a highly debatable question.

Fifth, accounting techniques continue to make exact determination of corporate tax levels extremely difficult. Congress should require uniformity in corporate accounting methods and perhaps consider legislation to require full and complete public disclosure of corporate tax returns.

Sixth, Congress must provide a national transportation tax policy. Railroads, poor profitmakers, paid much higher taxes than did the airlines — who are already benefactors of a wide range of Federal support and subsidization.

Seventh, "capital formation" proposals must be carefully considered, given the tendency for major American corporations to substantially sidestep or avoid U.S. Federal income taxes.

ABILITY TO DISCRIMINATE

Reprinted with permission from the Chicago Tribune-New York News Syndicate, Inc.

Usually difficult situations fail to present easy choices. Real life problems are too complex to permit simple choices between absolute right and wrong. The following exercise will test your ability to discriminate between degrees of truth and falsehood by completing the questionnaire. Circle the number on the continuum which most closely identifies your evaluation regarding each statement's degree of truth or falsehood.

1. Most untaxed income is in the middle and lower income brackets.

+
5	4	3	2	1	0	1	2	3	4	5
completely true			partially true			partially false			completely false	

 _

2. Any campaign to clean up the tax code is bound to deprive some powerful corporation of a cherished tax loophole.

+
5	4	3	2	1	0	1	2	3	4	5
completely true			partially true			partially false			completely false	

 _

3. The reason that everyone's taxes are too high is that government spending is too high.

+
5	4	3	2	1	0	1	2	3	4	5
completely true			partially true			partially false			completely false	

 _

4. The only tax reform which will help the average taxpayer is that which brings government spending under control.

+
5	4	3	2	1	0	1	2	3	4	5
completely true			partially true			partially false			completely false	

 _

5. Every year there are wealthy corporations that escape paying federal income taxes.

+
5	4	3	2	1	0	1	2	3	4	5
completely true			partially true			partially false			completely false	

 _

6. Because of loopholes, the 48 percent corporate tax rate is usually reduced to an average effective federal income tax rate of about 22 percent.

+
5	4	3	2	1	0	1	2	3	4	5
completely true			partially true			partially false			completely false	

 _

7. Most of the loopholes in our tax laws accrue not to the relatively rich, but to the relatively poor.

```
+   5  4  3  2  1  0  1  2  3  4  5   _
   completely   partially   partially   completely
      true        true        false       false
```

8. A flat 10 percent federal tax on all personal income would yield about as much revenue as the present tax rate scale that exempts half of the nation's taxable income through deductions and loopholes.

```
+   5  4  3  2  1  0  1  2  3  4  5   _
   completely   partially   partially   completely
      true        true        false       false
```

9. Cutting corporate taxes is the quickest way to put people back to work and create new jobs.

```
+   5  4  3  2  1  0  1  2  3  4  5   _
   completely   partially   partially   completely
      true        true        false       false
```

10. No one that is wealthy should avoid paying taxes.

```
+   5  4  3  2  1  0  1  2  3  4  5   _
   completely   partially   partially   completely
      true        true        false       false
```

11. The sales tax is a better way to raise government revenue than the income tax.

```
+   5  4  3  2  1  0  1  2  3  4  5   _
   completely   partially   partially   completely
      true        true        false       false
```

12. All income taxes should be of a progressive nature.

```
+   5  4  3  2  1  0  1  2  3  4  5   _
   completely   partially   partially   completely
      true        true        false       false
```

THE
NATIONAL
DEBT

AMERICA'S MOUNTAIN OF DEBT

The Plain Truth

The Plain Truth is published by Ambassador College in Pasadena, California. It deals with domestic and international issues and claims to be written in the "light of Bible understanding."

Use the following questions to assist your reading:

1. According to the article, what does the public and private debt amount to?
2. Why does the greatest danger lie in government borrowing?
3. How do you interpret the cartoon in the reading?

Bankruptcy for America's largest city is virtually certain; attention now turns to the mop-up operations.

But while everyone has focused his attention on the financial worms which have devoured the Big Apple, a far more menacing problem has gone relatively unnoticed: The *whole nation* is living beyond its means. The truth is the American economy sits on a mountainous pile of debt. Public and private debt now totals more than $2.8 trillion, about $13,000 for every man, woman, and child in the United States.

The total figures are so large as to be incomprehensible. But what is comprehensible and important is that the amount of money that consumers, banks, and corporations have on hand with which to meet their short-term, month-by-month debts is shrinking.

As more consumers lose the game of financial brinkmanship, they are filing for bankruptcy in record numbers. The Bankruptcy Division of the U.S. courts prognosticates that "bankruptcy filings for 1975 will break every record in the book," a total of more than 230,000.

Corporations are doing much the same thing. Currently, most corporations have on hand only enough money to pay off about half of their short-term debts. Before 1964, they had the money to pay off all their short-term debts and still have some left over.

Furthermore, the amount of cash on hand with which corporations meet the interest payments on past borrowing is trending steadily downward. What this means is that very few American companies will be able to do much borrowing in the years ahead. Yet the next decade is a time when American industry will need a tremendous infusion of new machines and equipment, just to maintain its productivity.

The banking community hasn't been immune from loose fiscal policies either. Since the beginning of the sixties, bankers have set aside their traditional cautious ways and made loans with abandon — in the process making an extraordinary number of bad loans. As the seventies began, many banks found that they had made the classic mistake of borrowing short, at high interest rates, and lending long, at low rates. The squeeze has

**'STEP UP EVERYBODY —
THE DRINKS ARE ON HIM'**

Editorial cartoon by Don Hesse
Copyright © 1976, St. Louis Globe Democrat
Reprinted with permission of Los Angeles Times Syndicate.

already contributed to the miserable state of the construction industry, which has had a hard time passing on high interest rates to prospective buyers.

BALLOONING GOVERNMENT DEBT

But the greatest danger of all lies in government borrowing. State and local government debt now exceeds $200 billion, while the federal government is in hock to the tune of over $606 billion.

DEFICIT SPENDING CAUSES INFLATION

There is one major cause of inflation in the United States as well as two other factors of somewhat lesser importance. The major cause, — one that almost all economists, liberal and conservative alike will agree upon, is a continuing long-term series of large deficits in our Federal Budget. In the period since the end of the Korean War over 20 years ago, the Federal Government has spent over 150 billion dollars more than it has taken in from the taxpayers of the nation in taxes and half of that huge deficit has occurred in the last five years.

Charles H. Smith, Jr., "Can Freedom Survive In America," **Vital Speeches**, March 1, 1975, p. 300.

The *interest* on the national debt alone — $36 billion — is more than the entire federal budget in 1948.

The federal budget deficit this year is $68 billion, money which will either have to come out of savings — and that means higher interest rates — or be printed up — and that means inflation. In fact, the only really substantial difference between New York City and the Federal government is that Washington can always crank up the printing presses in order to prevent a default.

The price of staving off a run of bankruptcies, either business or governmental, may well be a jarring dose of hyper-inflation. To prevent the financial dominoes from falling, the Federal Reserve will have no choice but to create more money out of thin air. If X can't pay Y, Y may not have the money to pay Z. Either everybody goes broke or the government floods the economy with paper dollars.

WRONG PHILOSOPHY

The ultimate responsibility for the debt pyramid —
and the inflation it generated — rests upon a "have-it-
now-pay-later" syndrome that came to permeate
American thought in the 1960s. The attitude was that a
country could enjoy economic growth without first producing the wealth from which those benefits could flow.
And when an expensive war was engaged in, the decision was made to buy the guns — but not to cut back on
the butter.

Now the realization that the economy isn't one big
rockcandy mountain is coming home. "Liberal" governors such as Michael Dukakis in Massachusetts and
Jerry Brown in California have turned fiscal conservatives. Brown, in fact, believes that the basic problem is
that there are finite limits to what government can do,
and that those limits have been reached.

Still, it may be too little, too late. California's Brown
speaks of human nature as "constant" and "weak" —
it is still susceptible to the something-for-nothing
demagoguery which manifests itself in government
budgets all out of proportion to what people are willing,
or able, to pay.

The late historian Arnold Toynbee, who died recently, feared that democracies would be unable to
cope with the economic cataclysms he foresaw lying
just ahead, and that, as a result, they would be replaced
by totalitarian regimes. New York has sown the wind. It
remains to be seen whether the whole nation will reap
the whirlwind.

NATIONAL DEBT: NOT A CRUSHING BURDEN

Walter W. Heller

Walter W. Heller is regents' professor of economics at the University of Minnesota. He is a leading liberal economist and has served as an economic advisor to the Johnson and Kennedy Administrations.

Keep the following questions in mind while you read:

1. How does the author say the government is depicted?
2. What does he claim are the five areas of misunderstanding?
3. Why does he say that the federal debt is not a crushing burden?

Excerpted from testimony by Walter W. Heller before the joint economic committee of Congress on February 6, 1976.

I am concerned over the distressing tendency in recent years to miseducate and, wittingly or unwittingly, mislead the American people on vital issues of economic policy and fact. This process, calculated or not, is contributing to misunderstanding of basic economic relationships, unnecessary anxiety on many fronts and a loss of faith in the American economy and its public institutions. Let me cite a few examples.

The federal government is depicted as expanding like some monstrous protoplasmic blob that threatens to snuff out economic freedom and initiative. Yet the facts will show that the federal budget as a proportion of gross national product held virtually steady at about 20 percent from 1953 to 1973. It is projected to rise to 21 percent in fiscal 1977 — but adjusted to a full-employment basis, the figure would be right back at 20 percent.

Or take the supposed "crushing burden of federal debt." A striking chart included in last year's budget documents (but omitted this year) shows that the federal debt held by the public dropped from 82 percent of annual GNP in 1950 to 26 percent in 1974. Seen in this perspective, the public debt is a far different and more manageable problem than the general impression abroad in the land.

A third area of widespread misapprehension centers on the large deficits in the federal budget. Here, two misimpressions are being fostered:

• The $70-billion to $75-billion deficit is being identified with profligacy in spending and fiscal irresponsibilty, when, in fact, it is almost entirely a hostage to recession. If we were operating at full employment, tax revenues would be $50 billion to $55 billion higher than they are; unemployment compensation would be about $15 billion lower, and other cyclically responsive outlays like food stamps, Medicare and Medicaid and pensions, would be about $5 billion lower.

So almost all of the deficit is a product of the recession. Ironically, the selfsame monetary and fiscal authorities whose disastrously tight policies in 1974 helped aggravate the recession, and hence the deficit, are the ones who are loudest in decrying it as an example of the lack of fiscal discipline.

• A related charge is that government deficits are the root of all inflationary evil. How is it, then, that inflation is ebbing in the face of the largest deficits in history?

> **The federal debt held by the public dropped from 82 percent of annual GNP in 1950 to 26 percent in 1974. Seen in this perspective, the public debt is a far different and more manageable problem than the general impression abroad in the land.**

A fourth area of anguished misapprehension relates to the Social Security system. The impression has been given that it is about to go broke. Again, the recession is partly the culprit in cutting revenues and increasing the flow of benefits. The financing problems of the Social Security system can clearly be met.

A fifth example is the mistaken belief that Congress is an instrument of irresponsible and loose spending — an impression that totally ignores the responsible new procedures and spending limits that it is observing. Indeed, the greater danger at the moment in the light of the economy's needs is that there might be excessive zeal in clamping a ceiling on government expenditures.

Finally, the continuing barrage of statements and studies — for example, the April 1, 1975, release by the Treasury entitled "U.S. Ranking in Investment and in Real Economic Growth Is Among Lowest of Industrialized Countries" — is giving the public a false image of the true strength of the American economy. Only the "fine print" brings out that U.S. productivity is still the best in the world, with even the high-growth countries like France and West Germany having achieved only 80 percent of the American level of productivity.

National leaders could in good grace put away their sackcloth and ashes and point with some pride to such comparative strengths of the U.S. economy as the following:

• The United States has been growing steadily more competitive, with its unit-labor costs rising only 10 percent from 1970 to 1974, while Canada's (with the next-best performance) rose 29 percent, West Germany's 90 percent and Japan's 100 percent.

• Correspondingly, U.S. manufacturing exports held up remarkably well in the face of world-wide recession in 1975, and the U.S. dollar is still the most sought-after currency in the world.

To be candid about economic shortcomings and government problems is a virtue. But to denigrate the U.S. economy and exaggerate its problems and mis-identify their sources is certainly a vice. The sooner policy-makers talk economic sense instead of nonsense to the American people, the better our chances will be of coping with the truly tough problems we face.

CAUSE AND EFFECT
RELATIONSHIPS

Reprinted with permission from the Chicago Tribune-
New York News Syndicate, Inc.

149

This discussion exercise provides practice in the skill of analyzing cause and effect relationships. Causes of human conflict and social problems are usually very complex. The following statements indicate possible causes for what many believe is a national debt and an annual federal budget deficit that are too high. Rank the statements by assigning the number (1) to the most important cause, number (2) to the second most important, and so on until the ranking is finished. Omit any statements that you feel are not causative factors. Add any causes you think have been left out. Then discuss and compare your decisions with other class members.

_____ a. The military budget

_____ b. Money given to undeserving welfare recipients

_____ c. Medicaid

_____ d. Local school budgets

_____ e. Tax deductions and loopholes for the rich

_____ f. Tax deductions and loopholes for the poor

_____ g. The Health, Education and Welfare budget

_____ h. Foreign economic aid programs

_____ i. Foreign military aid programs

_____ j. The Social Security program

_____ k. The Postal Service

CHAPTER 6

SOCIAL SECURITY

SOCIAL SECURITY IS GOING BROKE

M. Stanton Evans

M. Stanton Evans is a columnist for the Los Angeles Times Syndicate and a radio commentator on the CBS program, "Spectrum." A former managing editor of **Human Events** and for 14 years the editor of the **Indianapolis News**, Evans has been chairman of the American Conservative Union since 1971.

While reading use the following questions as a guide:

1. Why does the author say Social Security is being destroyed?
2. Does the cartoon in this reading support the author's ideas?

M. Stanton Evans, "Big Spenders Are Destroying Social Security," **Human Events**, February 7, 1976, p. 8. Reprinted with permission from **Human Events**.

A standard rap against economy-minded folk who try to cut the federal budget is that they are secretly out to "destroy" Social Security.

The charge is silly but effective — as witness the damage done to Sen. Barry Goldwater back in 1964. Its political utility is obvious: Since so many people are dependent on Social Security, the merest hint that it will be abandoned is enough to start a political panic. Reasoned discussion of the issue is therefore crushed to earth before it can get started.

This method of proceeding is doubly ironic, since it is just such emotional demagogy that is "destroying" Social Security. And make no mistake that it is being destroyed. Its untouchable and virtually undiscussable status means the politicos have cheerfully piled on the spending hikes across the years, incurring stupendous obligations for the future. Now the bills are falling due, and the system is flat broke.

Just how broke can be attested by U.S. citizens who started paying Social Security taxes at the turn of the year. For anyone earning upwards of $13,100, these taxes have increased again — up by 8.5 per cent in certain cases. This means that payroll taxes have grown by 47 per cent since 1973, to a crushing maximum rate of $1,790 a year (counting employer and employe contributions together.)

That prodigious tax bite also means the average American is forking over more in Social Security taxes than he is in income taxes. And the problem is going to get worse. Under increases already programmed into law, Social Security taxes will reach $2,360 per person by 1980. In another 20 years, the maximum bite will be a mind-boggling $6,772 — and there is no likelihood that even this will make the program solvent.

These problems have developed because the program was so heavily frontloaded: Those who entered the system early on received entitlement to benefits far in excess of their own taxes, but since there were more youthful taxpayers than retirees, the system's income exceeded payments rather comfortably. As late as 1945, the payouts amounted to only a third of a billion dollars.

HEADED
FOR TROUBLE

Without some strong medicine, Social Security is headed for trouble. Already, it's living from hand to mouth, and may soon be in the red. Officials in the know are the ones most concerned.

"Social Security," **U.S. News & World Report**, July 15, 1974, p. 26.

Now, however, all that is reversed: Successive waves of retirees have entered the system, and are drawing benefits repeatedly enlarged by Congress. Annual payments have accordingly zoomed — to $10 billion in 1960, and better than $70 billion today. Birthrates, meantime, have fallen sharply, reducing the number of youthful taxpayers relative to the elderly. Result: A yawning gap between the system's obligations and ability to pay.

As of June 30, 1973, the unfunded obligation of the system was an incredible $2.1 trillion, and there have of course been many entrants to the program since then. This compares to a Social Security "trust fund" of $43 billion or thereabouts, which consists of government promises to pay itself, and which in any event is being depleted by annual operating losses.

Charles D. Hobbs and Stephen Powlesland observe in their useful study, **Retirement Security Reform** (published by the Institute for Liberty and Community, Concord, Vt.):

> "The Social Security trust fund, once intended to grow until the benefit obligations were fully funded has, in the face of increasing benefits, rapidly dwindled to a cash-flow account, at the current rate of spending and income, will run out of money by 1980 or soon afterward, according to Social Security Administration actuaries. Payroll taxes paid into Social Security are presently paid out in benefits within less than a year...."

154

SOCIAL SECURITY WILL BRING NATIONAL CRISIS

The real long-term crisis will come if the social security expansionists continue to have their way and social security replaces instead of supplements other retirement programs. As the cost of social security increases [and the Social Security Administration projects an increase from the present 11.9 percent of taxable income to 22.44 percent] other pension programs will be phased out. Those pension programs that are not totally funded during the working lifetime of the present employee will face an acute funding crisis because future workers will not be willing to contribute to a plan paying them nothing and employers will be spending their fringe benefit funds on social security tax.

When this happens our country will face another crisis unprecedented in our history. Pension and other retirement programs now own about 40 percent of American industry. Money from these programs represents the only major growing supply of capital to finance private research and productive facilities. Drying up this source of capital threatens survival of our economic system.

Mel Hansen, Minnesota State Senator, letter to the editor in **The Christian Science Monitor** of July 19, 1976. Reprinted by permission from **The Christian Science Monitor** © The Christian Science Publishing Society. All Rights reserved.

It is to overcome this horrendous deficit that Social Security tax rates are raised again and again. Between 1940 and 1974, the benefits afforded by the system rose 640 per cent, which sounds pretty good until we compare it to the contemporary tax rise. When we examine that particular table, we find that Social Security levies in this span increased by 2,474 per cent — excluding the hikes that have recently gone into effect, and those proposed by President Ford.

Hobbs and Powlesland provide us with the table which appears on this page.

The simple truth of the matter is that Social Security is on the rocks, put there by the people who claim to be its most devoted friends. The "destroyers" of the system are precisely those political spendthrifts who insist on making its mounting fiscal problems worse.

TOTAL U.S. DEBT:

ON ITS WAY TOWARD THREE TRILLION DOLLARS

$.606 — 1954
$1.15 — 1964
$2.8 — 1975

IN TRILLIONS

READING 24

SOCIAL SECURITY IS A-OK

Paul A. Samuelson

Paul A. Samuelson is a prominent liberal economist who has written in many scholarly and popular journals about domestic and international economic issues.

Think of the following questions while you read:

1. Why does the author say Social Security has a clean bill of health?
2. What does he claim are some needed improvements?

As the age of 40 nears, a thoroughgoing health checkup is in order. Our social-security system for old-age-retirement pensions, started in 1937 under FDR, has been going for 38 years. Fears have been expressed that it is becoming actuarially unsound; and, much worse, that at some time in the future, it will become bankrupt and be unable to pay the pensions so desperately needed and which people have earned the right to expect.

We have just had two independent audits. One is by the thirteen-person Social Security Advisory Council, consisting of representatives of the general public, labor, management, and the self-employed. Chaired by W. Allen Wallis, chancellor of the University of Rochester, this includes a fair example of Establishment leaders and is, if anything, weighted on the conservative side.

The other is by the Panel on Social Security Financing, appointed by 1974 Senate resolution and charged with giving "...an expert, independent analysis of the actuarial status of the social-security system." Chaired by William C. L. Hsiao of the Harvard School of Public Health, who is both an actuary and an economist, it includes three other actuaries and two other economists. If the actuaries have reputations for excellence and fairmindedness in their profession matching that of the economists in my profession, the Hsiao panel inspires confidence and serves as a valuable second opinion to supplement the Wallis council's checkup on social-security health.

CLEAN BILL OF HEALTH

The clinical findings are favorable. The patient is sound with a life expectancy that can be measured in the centuries. Both authorities agree.

To be sure, there are some minor defects in need of attention, so to speak, like a mole that might become serious if not attended to. Retired participants have their pensions indexed, to protect them from inflation. The formula is a proper one. But the way that earners who are not yet retired have their stipends computed is defective and could result after years of inflation in an inequitable and burdensome benefit cost. Just as there are alternative ways of treating an undesirable mole, so there are alternative ways of correcting the arithmetic of pre-retirement indexing: both groups recommend immediate attention to this matter.

NO IMMEDIATE CRISIS

In brief, the Social Security program — meaning the cash benefits of the Old Age, Survivors and Disability Insurance system [OASDI] — does have serious financial problems. They are both short-range and long-range. But although the short-run situation is serious, there will be no immediate cash-flow crisis in the next two or three years.

Robert J. Myers, "Social Security: Don't Push The Panic Button," **America**, September 20, 1975, p. 140.

The basic problem facing the social-security system is that its financing must take account of present declining birth rates, increasing years of life expectancy in retirement, productivity trends in the economy and plausible ranges of average inflation. Using the most reasonable guesses on these trends, one finds that the now-scheduled timing of tax changes and benefits will by the end of the 1980s threaten to deplete the so-called trust fund set up for social security. There is nothing new about this finding, which has been familiar to experts for years. However, the Hsaio panel estimates, which seem more realistic than those of the Wallis council, suggest that in 50 years the cost of the program, relative to total payrolls, will double to 20 per cent from the present 10 per cent. This is a sharp revision of previous official projections.

NEEDED IMPROVEMENTS

What ought to be done to restore the system to the pink of health? For the present, nothing *has* to be done: but both groups believe that it would be well to plan *now* to augment revenues.

Remarkable indeed is the general recommendation of the Wallis council, subject to some dissents but still commanding a majority of this nonradical group, that *some recourse be made to general tax revenues of the Treasury rather than continue to rely exclusively on payroll taxing of prospective recipients*. This is a bold stand that, on reflection, I endorse. What is important is the principle. What is less crucial is the specific recommendation of the council that it be the hospital-insurance part of the medicare program that be put on the general taxpayers' shoulders.

The present system is neither fish nor fowl, but it *is* good red herring. Unlike private insurance, this is a case of social insurance in which the premiums levied on workers do not suffice to finance future benefits fully. But still there is adherence to the principle that benefits are to be related to earnings; and every earner is given the feeling that the benefits received are deserved by right.

Continued good health requires continued changes. Eventually we shall have comprehensive health insurance. And before that, I pray, a fairer deal for women.

READING 25

SOCIAL SECURITY SHOULD BE MANDATORY

Sylvia Porter

Sylvia Porter is a nation-
ally syndicated column-
ist. She writes daily
columns on economic
and social issues.

Use the following questions to assist your reading:

1. Why does Sylvia Porter say Social Security is more
   than a pension program?
2. Why does she say some cities want to pull out of
   the Social Security program?
3. What advantages does she see for cities that rema
   in the program?

Sylvia Porter, **Minneapolis Tribune**, May 5, and May 6, 1976.''Your
Money's Worth'' by Sylvia Porter, courtesy of Field Newspaper
Syndicate.

Though dying of leukemia, police officer John Orlando continued to patrol his beat in San Francisco in the hope that he would last long enough to qualify his wife and four children for death benefits that would equal one-third his salary. But Orlando died a few weeks ago, two months, 16 days short of his goal of 10 years on the force. Under the police pension plan, his family was eligible to collect only a lump sum death benefit.

The tale would have been different if California had exercised its option to provide Orlando and his fellow officers with Social Security coverage as an underlying base for their civil service pension program. With Social Security credit for as little as a year and a half out of the three years before death, a young worker's widow and children can be paid regular monthly Social Security benefits until the children are grown.

Payments to a family with three or more members now range from $152.10 to more than $900 a month, depending on the average covered earnings of the deceased worker. And these payments will increase 6.4 percent starting in July.

Social Security (unlike pension programs generally) is not just a retirement program. It is also a massive group life and disability program, providing protection for the family during all the years before the worker retires — as well as after. Moreover, it provides health insurance for the elderly and those who become disabled, when the health coverage they may have had at work ends.

In contrast, some public pension programs do not pay survivors' benefits at all. Those that do require much longer periods of coverage than Social Security and they pay less.

As a long-time resident of New York, I sympathize with the city's financial problems and recognize that it wants to pull out of Social Security to save the money it now pays in Social Security taxes. I also know that New York City's civil service workers have a generous pension plan. And Mayor Abraham Beame's estimate that New York would save $200 million annually if it did not have to pay the employer's share of the Social Security tax is impressive.

Other financially troubled governments are making similar threats. And it should be understood that any state or municipality has a choice about paying Social Security taxes because the U.S. Constitution provides that the federal government cannot tax a state without the state's permission. As a result, 30 percent of state and local government employees are outside the Social Security system.

Would the savings that Mayor Beame projects be as large as he suggests? Not if New York undertook to provide its employees with some form of disability insurance. And not if it tried to provide some range of survivors benefits plus potential medical protection for the elderly similar to what most Americans get under Social Security. Then, an estimated $50 million bite for disability insurance alone would be taken out of the $200 million a year saving projected for New York City.

The temptation to save on Social Security also is luring other municipalities to the same "solution." And once out of the system, following a two-year notice of termination, the state or local government that withdraws could never bring its employees back under Social Security unless a special act of Congress permitted the return....

So, should New York and other troubled cities withdraw their employees from Social Security? Or should the cities cut back on their own pension plans and stay under Social Security?

"Stay in Social Security, cut back on your own pension plan," concludes Robert Tilove, a pension expert who has just published a comprehensive study "Public Employe Pension Funds," commissioned by the Twentieth Century Fund. Social Security, he emphasizes, should be mandatory for all public employees — federal, state and local — just as it is mandatory for all workers in private enterprise.

Government pension plans should be integrated with Social Security, so that public employees do not have top-heavy retirement protection due to the combination of Social Security with their own pension plans. The staff pension plans should be redesigned so

163

that they take into account increases in Social Security benefits in recent years.

Under no circumstances should employees be allowed net retirement incomes that are higher than their take-home pay just before they retired.

City workers with 10 years of Social Security coverage would still retain the right to Social Security benefits, without paying another cent in taxes. "Millions of dolars in benefits" would be paid out to these workers — but financed largely by other workers and their employers. Meanwhile, most city employees with less than 10 years under Social Security would lose their rights to future benefits (unless they took covered jobs after retirement or moonlighted.)

Social Security [unlike pension programs generally] is not just a retirement program. It is also a massive group life and disability program, providing protection for the family during all the years before the worker retires — as well as after. Moreover, it provides health insurance for the elderly and those who become disabled, when the health coverage they may have had at work ends.

Key advantages of making Social Security the primary source of income protection for the nation's workers:

• Social Security covers 9 out of 10 jobs and the credits you earn move with you from job to job.

• Your benefits are protected by the entire economy, do not rely on the financial health of a single municipality, state or firm.

• Social Security can be readily financed so that the program is kept up to date with living costs and wage increases.

• Benefits are tax-free. Other retirement benefits become taxable as soon as the employee has collected an amount equal to his contributions to the plan.

• No other program provides the extent of family protection you get under Social Security: Income and health insurance protection in your older years, protection for your family in case of your death or disability.

SOCIAL SECURITY SHOULD BE OPTIONAL

William Murchison

William Murchison is an editorial writer and columnist for **The Dallas Morning News**. He has authored numerous articles and book reviews in conservative periodicals.

Use the following questions to help your understanding of the reading:

1. How does the author characterize Sylvia Porter's view of human nature?
2. Why does Mr. Murchison think OASDI should be optional?
3. How do you interpret the cartoon in this reading?

William Murchison, "Sylvia Porter Can Have The Social Security Mess," **Human Events**, April 17, 1976, p. 11. Reprinted with permission.

At last the awful truth is out: Sylvia Porter does not believe that most of us have bat brains — neither those, nor the right to look after our own futures.

What ails the lady, you will ask? Plenty ails her. In her consumer column she has of late been trying to persuade us that the Social Security system, as it presently stands, is in robust shape. It is the journalistic equivalent of persuading Noah that all this drizzle will end in a moment.

Given that, as Mrs. Porter herself admits, the Social Security system owes more money than it can presently pay, she is understandably touchy.

Perhaps that is why she rounds on those who make "vicious attacks" on the system — who suggest outlandishly that a man should enjoy the right to invest his Social Security deduction in stocks, bonds or private annuities.

Mrs. Porter is shocked. Fancy giving the peasants the right to provide for their own futures! "Even with the best of intentions," she proclaims from Olympus, "Millions of you simply would not set aside money regularly..." Therefore, in our twilight years, we would end up on the welfare rolls — burdens on the state and on our fellow taxpayes.

Even if we did invest faithfully, says Mrs. Porter, we would be the losers. "You would not find a private insurance policy providing the comprehensive package of protection you now get from Social Security: retirement insurance, disability insurance, life insurance, health insurance for your older years..." As for investments, "most of you would end up short of your goal or wiped out."

Whoever said that it is conservatives whose opinion of human nature is the lowest? Mrs. Porter, a certified defender of the bureaucratic-collectivist order, wrinkles her nose more disparagingly at human capabilities than any Ronald Reagan ever has. Mrs. Porter thinks we cannot be trusted with our own money. We must trust the government instead.

Which is of course what we have done since the incipience of Social Security in 1935. And what has been the result? There is, for one thing, as Mrs. Porter reassures us, some $44 billion to $45 billion in the Social Security trust fund. The problem is that this is an emergency fund, and we are drawing on it even now. The Social Security system, in short, owes more money that it presently is taking in.

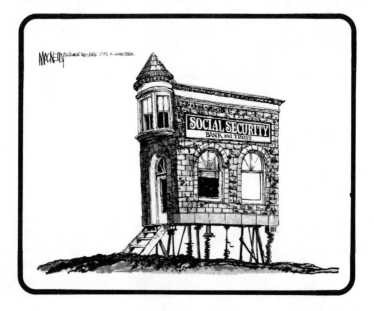

Reprinted with permission from the Chicago Tribune-New York News Syndicate, Inc.

To keep the system solvent we either will have to raise taxes sharply or hold down the increase in benefits. Neither approach is exactly palatable. The first hurts present workers; the second hurts those who have come to depend on Social Security to maintain their living standard in the face of inflation.

But what if we do nothing? By approximately 1980, the trust fund will be depleted. Because of the falling birthrate, moreover, the Social Security system's own trustees predict that by 2030, 100 workers will be supporting 50 beneficiaries. The present ratio is 100 to 30.

The Social Security System, as one can readily see, is no pension plan; it is a system of transfer payments — out of one pocket into another.

As a better economist than Mrs. Porter — to wit, Milton Friedman — has written, "An individual working person is in no sense building his own protection — as a person who contributes to a private vested pension system is building his own protection. Persons now receiving benefits are receiving much more than the actuarial value of the taxes that were paid on their behalf. Young persons are now being promised much less than the actuarial value of the taxes that are being paid on their behalf."

That is the system Mrs. Porter likes so very much.

As to one thing, the lady is right: The system must be maintained; it cannot be torn down. Too many Americans have come to depend on the government's assurances that the money will be there for them.

But Sylvia Porter notwithstanding, must the system always be run as it is run now? The "vicious attacks" Mrs. Porter so deplores are merely hardheaded suggestions that Americans should receive the right to decide where their money can best be invested. Perhaps, pragmatically speaking, the government must continue to require that we make such investments. But where is the sense in dragooning every worker into a "retirement plan" that is built on promises and paper?

Let Sylvia Porter reap the blessings of Social Security if she so wishes. Other Americans would greatly appreciate the freedom to take their trade elsewhere.

EXERCISE **6**

DISTINGUISHING BIAS FROM REASON

One of the most important critical thinking skills is the ability to distinguish between opinions based on emotions or bias and conclusions based on a rational consideration of facts. This discussion exercise is designed to promote experimentation with one's capacity to recognize biased statements.

Some of the following statements have been taken from Chapter Six and some have other origins. Consider each statement carefully. Mark (R) for any statement you feel is based on a rational consideration of the facts. Mark (B) for any statement you believe is based on prejudice, emotion or bias. Mark (I) for any statement you think is impossible to judge. Then discuss and compare your judgments with other class members.

R = A STATEMENT BASED ON REASON
B = A STATEMENT BASED ON BIAS
I = A STATEMENT IMPOSSIBLE TO JUDGE

_____ 1. The Social Security system is going broke.

_____ 2. Liberal politicians are out to buy votes with their irresponsible fiscal policies.

_____ 3. Conservatives are less concerned about the wage earners than the liberals.

_____ 4. Social Security is a sound system with a future that can be measured in centuries.

_____ 5. The liberal politicians are out to destroy Social Security with their spendthrift ways.

_____ 6. Social Security should be a mandatory program.

_____ 7. Conservatives wish to hold back raises in Social Security payments and are in general not very sympathetic to the needs of the elderly.

_____ 8. Unlike private retirement pension programs, Social Security is also a massive group life and disability program, and it provides health insurance for the elderly and the disabled.

_____ 9. People should not expect the government to provide for their retirement.

_____ 10. It is largely because of our large minority populations that we need a massive federal retirement program like Social Security.

_____ 11. Most people would rather build their own retirement program than be forced to have money deducted from every check for Social Security taxes.

CHAPTER **7**

MULTINATIONAL CORPORATIONS

READING 27

MULTINATIONALS
FOSTER INEQUALITY

Richard J. Barnet

Richard J. Barnet is co-director of the Institute for Policy Studies and is co-author of **Global Reach: The Power of Multinational Corporations.**

Consider the following questions while reading:

1. In what ways does the author say multinationals have a negative influence on poor nations?
3. Does the cartoon in this reading relate to any of the author's ideas?

Richard J. Barnet, ''Multinationals: A Dissenting View,'' **Saturday Review**, February 7, 1976, pp. 11, 12. Reprinted with permission.

Strong evidence indicates that the transformation of the world economy spearheaded by the multinationals is having an adverse impact on at least 60 percent of the world's population in three crucial aspects. First, the multinational corporation is undermining the ability of governments everywhere, including the United States, to maintain employment, to protect the money supply, to prevent the erosion of the tax base, and thus to meet essential social needs for a majority of their citizens. Second, it is promoting a model of development and a world distribution system that increases inequalities across the planet — widening the gap between rich and poor. Finally, following a narrow balance-sheet definition of efficiency and a grow-or-die philosophy, it is misusing and misallocating resources.

MULTINATIONALS IN THE UNDERDEVELOPED COUNTRIES

In the underdeveloped world, where most of the global population lives, there are real conflicts of interest between a global corporation and a poor country. The corporation is obviously interested in minimizing taxes, reducing its labor costs, moving its capital freely, and minimizing local controls. But the consequences for the poor country are often disastrous: loss of foreign exchange (Columbia lost $20 million in one year from overpricing in the drug industry alone); loss of tax revenues; preemption of local capital (during the Sixties about 78 percent of the manufacturing operations of U.S.-based global corporations were financed from local capital); and unemployment.

Sufficient evidence has now been collected by international agencies, government studies, and independent scholars to indicate that corporations frequently take advantage of their superior bargaining power in underdeveloped societies in ways that keep poor countries poor. Overpricing in the drug industry has been scandalous. For example, U.S. drug companies have "charged" their subsidiaries in Colombia 82 times the international market price. Such "transfer pricing," which, for many different industries, has also been documented in Chile, Peru, Ecuador, Pakistan, Iran, the Philippines, and elsewhere, has the effect of siphoning capital from poor countries.

Multinationals dominate the crucial process of transfer of technology to poor countries. By engaging in what the United Nations calls "restrictive business practices," agreements that prohibit the country from using the technology for its own exports, the multinationals perpetuate a relationship of technological dependence. (It is worth noting that the two countries that have developed dramatically in the last 100 years — the United States and Japan — have kept control of their technology even when they obtained financing from abroad.)

MAXIMIZING PROFITS

We already know enough to begin to cope with all the major problems that now threaten human life and much of the rest of the life on the Earth. Our crisis is not a crisis of information but a crisis of decision, of policy. We live with the myth that if only our governments had the proper information, it would be used, it would be acted upon. But that is not the world in which we live.

Though we already know enough to cope with all our major problems, however, I don't know one of those major problems that we can begin to cope with while maximizing profits. And a society like our own, which puts the maximization of profits above all other considerations, is therefore heading for destruction....

In what we fondly call the "free world" — that phrase used to trouble me until I realized that it meant those nations which get their armaments free from the United States — the governments are in reality not the masters but the servants. Then who are the masters? I believe our so-called free world is now wholly controlled by such multi-national super-enterprises as General Motors, Exxon, the Chase Manhattan Bank, ITT, Dutch Shell, and British Petroleum.

George Wald, "There Isn't Much Time," **The Progressive**, December, 1975, p. 22.

175

The transfer of technology by multinationals is having serious disruptive effects because to a substantial extent it is the wrong technology. Extending the useful life of capital-intensive technology developed for the United States makes sense for the corporation but not for the country. Labor-saving technology in agriculture, the construction industry, and manufacturing is destroying jobs and accelerating the unemployment process. Despite a dramatic increase in the importance of the manufacturing sector to the Latin American economy, it employs a slightly smaller percentage of the total work force than it did 50 years ago.

Although it is true that global corporations in low-wage areas in Taiwan, Hong Kong, Haiti, Mexico, and elsewhere are creating jobs for thousands of workers, the dollar-a-day "labor aristocracy" is a small fraction of the local population; the development model of the multinational corporations does not benefit the majority of the country's population either as workers or as consumers. Such countries as Mexico and Brazil, which have dramatically increased their gross national product through foreign investment by multinational corporations, have suffered increasing concentration of income largely as a result of mounting unemployment. In the early Fifties the richest 20 percent of the Mexican population had 10 times the income of the poorest 20 percent. After 10 years of rapid industrial growth, sparked primarily by the multinationals, the rich had substantially increased their share. The same trend is observable in Brazil. As Brazil's President Emilio Medici once put it, "Brazil is doing well, but the people are not."

The point is not that the multinationals are responsible for poverty in the Third World — that is a complex story in which foreign economic and political exploitation is an important but not sufficient explanation — but that their development model, while it rescues a few, perpetuates poverty for the many. The development model of the multinational corporations calls for a worldwide distribution system of standardized goods, a "Global Shopping Center" to serve affluent enclaves across the planet. But a profit-dominated global distribution system diverts resources from the places where they are most needed (poor countries and poor regions of rich countries) to those where they are least needed (rich countries and rich regions).

The role of the multinational corporation as world distributors is most dramatic in the area of food. Agribusiness is now buying or renting more and more arable land. Decisions on what to plant and where to distribute the harvest are made with the balance sheet in mind. (Corporate managers who attempt to run their firms like foundations are likely to end up in one.) Thus, it is profitable in poor countries to use land for exportable luxury crops even while the people are suffering severe malnutrition because it does not grow enough grain. (In Colombia a hectare of wheat brings 12,500 pesos; carnations for export bring a million.) Global corporations further complicate the dietary problem in poor countries by fostering what the nutritionist Derrick B. Jelliffe calls "commerciogenic malnutrition." According to Albert Stridsberg in **Advertising Age**: "It has long been known that in the poorest regions of Mexico where soft drinks play a functional role in the diet, it is the international brands — Coke and Pepsi — not local off-brands, which dominate. Likewise, a Palestinian-refugee urchin, shining shoes in Beirut saves his piastres for a real Coca-Cola, at twice the price of a local cola." Company campaigns have succeeded in increasing consumption of white bread, confections, and soft drinks among the poorest people in the world by convincing them that status, convenience, and a sweet taste are more important than nutrition.

THE DEVELOPMENT MODEL OF MULTINATIONALS

The development model of the multinationals — centralized planning for global-profit maximization — is also causing instability in the United States and other industrialized countries. U.S.-based global companies, many of which now derive more than 50 percent of their profits from abroad, do not have the same stake in the United States as a traditional American company does. (The vice-chairman of Mobil, according to the **Washington Post**, recently threatened to move out of the United States if foreign tax credits for oil companies are eliminated.)

Our tax laws, our labor laws, our laws for protecting the money supply — in short, the basic tools for promoting economic stability — are all premised on the existence of a national economy that can be more or less effectively managed within the continental limits of the

United States. But the ability of corporations to shift production and to move capital has brought about a globalization of the economy that has made that assumption obsolete. The U.S. economy is now the North American division of the world economy. Because there are no effective world public authorities, no community-based planning in the United States, the managers of the multinationals in their daily operations have by default become the principal planners for the U.S. economy.

MULTINATIONAL COMPANIES

Justus in the **Minneapolis Star**. Reprinted with permission from the **Minneapolis Star**.

178

We are beginning to see some of the same adverse consequences of concentrated power that we have seen for many years in underdeveloped countries. The tax base is eroding. Because of the use of such devices as Gulf Oil's dummy corporation in the Bahamas, the global giants have been able to shift a substantial portion of their tax burden onto the middle class. In 1958 corporations were contributing more than 25 percent of federal revenues; by 1973, less than 15 percent. In 1969 the largest 100 corporations paid at a rate of 26.9 percent, but average corporations paid at a rate of 44 percent.

The export of production to cheap labor sites abroad has created a major employment crisis in such basic industries as rubber, electronics, textiles, and automobiles. For example, Ford and General Motors were increasing their investments in their foreign plants even as they were laying off tens of thousands of workers in Detroit. And Ford's plant in Valencia, Spain, is planning to produce thousands of compacts for import into the United States. The threat to move out of the country has eroded labor's bargaining power. A corporation can neutralize the effects of a strike by shifting production to its plants in countries, such as Taiwan, that advertise their strike-free labor force. There is a connection between the loss of unskilled and semi-skilled jobs and the loss of labor's bargaining power and the "slow but persistent trend toward inequality" of income that Peter Henle of the Library of Congress noted in 1972. (In the last three years, according to the Department of Labor, real wages of workers, excluding agriculture, have declined at least 8.7 percent.)

MULTINATIONS ARE OLIGOPOLIES

The multinationals are, virtually without exception, oligopolies. Four firms, or even fewer, dominate the market in automobiles, packaged foods, tires, computers, and other basic items. Oligopolies seldom compete in terms of price, and the absence of effective price competition is inflationary. But, more important, the power to dominate markets is easily translated into the power to dominate politics. The energy companies, for example, have been the energy planners for the society. Until recently, their goal — and that of the automotive industry as well — has been the promotion of energy-guzzling technology. Their definition of progress has been the displacement of human energy, of which we have a surplus, with fossil fuels, of which we have a shortage — all of which may have been good short-term corporate planning, but it is not good social planning. A disparity is discernible between strategies for producing good quarterly statements and strategies for developing societies.

CONCLUSIONS

It is too much to expect the managers of global corporations to subordinate their strategies to the public interest without changing the legal and political ground rules under which corporations operate. The excessive power of large corporations over the political and economic life of this country has all but destroyed the system of checks and balances in our society. We need new policies to stop the unending process of conglomeration and merger, to end the small taxpayer's subsidization of the large corporations, and to revise the built-in bias in our laws against small business and free competition. We need to give communities the legal power to protect themselves from the runaway shop. We need laws that realistically differentiate the global corporation from the corner drugstore. Having amassed so much power that whole communities are dependent upon it, the global corporation is not just another piece of private property. It is a social institution and should be treated as one.

We need to revitalize our political institutions so that they keep pace with the revolutionary changes that have taken place in our economy. Without such institutions for increased community control of the economy, the multinationals will continue to exercise unaccountable power. The redistribution of economic and political power is the price of maintaining democracy in America.

READING

MULTINATIONALS PROMOTE ECONOMIC GROWTH

F. Perry Wilson

F. Perry Wilson is Chairman of the Board of Union Carbide Corporation. He is also director of the Manufacturers Hanover Trust Company, Manufacturers Hanover Corporation, The Continental Corporation and the A.O. Smith Corporation.

As you read try to answer the following questions:

1. Why does a company become multinational, according to the author?
2. Why does he say the multinationals are viewed with distrust?
3. What contributions to the world's economic growth does Mr. Wilson say the Multinationals have made?

F. Perry Wilson, "Confessions of a Confirmed Capitalist," **Vital Speeches**, October 1, 1975, pp. 755-57. Reprinted with permission from **Vital Speeches Of The Day**.

The "one world" dreamed of by philosophers and conquerors as diverse in outlook and in time as Saint Augustine, Marx, Alexander the Great, and Napoleon is now much closer to reality. The United States and other nations are dependent on each other in terms of trade, technology, capital, and natural resources. This interdependence is recognized by most nations. The Tokyo Declaration of 1973 opening the current round of trade talks, the agreement of the oil consuming nations to pool supplies, the Bucharest conference on food and population, all reflect various aspects of new economic realities.

A CREATIVE INTERNATIONAL INSTITUTION

One of the centerpieces of our economic development is the multi-national corporation. As Daniel Moynihan has stated it is arguably the most creative international institution of the 20th Century. This is not to say that a multi-national has some special claim on creativity. It does not. The creativity that Moynihan has in mind consists primarily of the multi-national's recognition of, and its response to, the historical realities and opportunities of the post-World War II period. I submit that the development of the multi-national corporation is a natural and productive one in the economic environment of our times.

Essentially, a company becomes a multi-national because it has developed technologies, products and services that provide better values in meeting the needs of international markets. This involves a relationship that must be mutually beneficial and therefore to the self-interest of both the host country and to the multi-national corporation.

What makes up the pragmatic awareness of self-interest of a nation? It may be the creation of new jobs, it may contribute to the balance of payment position of the host country, it may upgrade the natural resources of the country, or in other ways improve the standard of living of its people. The multi-national's presence might produce one or all of these effects. In the process, however, the multi-national corporation must abide by local laws and customs. Otherwise, whatever good its presence in a host country produces would be canceled and replaced by a hostile political climate that would make it difficult for any foreign corporation to function effectively in that nation.

The other side of this self-interest concept is the motivation of the multi-national corporation. As with any profit-making enterprise, it exists to make a return on its investment on a long-term basis. I hasten to emphasize that there is no contradiction between this profit-making objective and the beneficial effect the corporation has on a host country's economy.

To illustrate this interrelationship, let me cite an example from Union Carbide's experience. For many years, Union Carbide had been manufacturing a range of products in India that saved the country a substantial amount of foreign exchange. Otherwise, these products would have had to be imported. Nevertheless, there was a need for some foreign exchange to purchase certain raw materials and equipment that were not available from Indian sources.

Union Carbide sought new ways to balance this need. Our investigations turned up the fact that waters surrounding India were rich in large and high-quality shrimp for which there were large markets in the United States, Europe, and Japan. After considerable development work, trawlers and shore facilities were designed and built employing novel and efficient freezing and processing techniques. The harvesting, packaging, and distribution of shrimp to foreign markets is now an on-going and profitable business. Equally important, the foreign exchange being earned by this new venture is most welcome as India struggles with her balance of payments problems.

To be sure, not many problems involving international trade are solved so deftly. Yet, I do believe that this example serves to illustrate the creative role that the multi-national corporation can and does play in the economic growth of nations, especially in the third world.

REASONS FOR DISTRUST

Why, then, are multi-national corporations viewed with such hostility and distrust? The reasons, I fear, are a mixed bag of generalized accusations, half-truths, outright myths, and, most importantly, the failure on the part of many multi-national corporations to explain adequately their role in international trade.

This is a new and complex era in international economic relations and, unfortunately, it is not fully understood by many people in this country and around the world. As a result, it is all too easy to blame the multi-national corporation for employment, inflation, recission, and trade deficits. The reasons are simple enough. The multi-national offers a highly visible and tempting political target.

THE INTERNATIONAL CORPORATION

- Today's international corporation is not just a manufacturer but the greatest self-help institution yet devised;

- It is not just an employer but the world's most effective training laboratory;

- It is the most effective instrument yet developed for the creation of goods and services to meet human needs;

- It has proved its ability to build the basic structures of society, create jobs, generate income, pay taxes, transfer funds and technology, and raise living and health standards;

- It has forged ahead of governments in the ability to deal with concrete problems across national frontiers and boundaries;

- It is building solid working alliances among men and nations at a speed and on a scale dwarfing other international organizations and movements;

- Yet it is under attack and, in many countries, struggling just to survive.

"Top Management Report On Government-Business Cooperation in the Field of International Public Affairs," International Management and Development Institute, 2600 Virginia Avenue, N.W., Suite 905, Washington, D.C. 20037.

The disclosures of bribes and illegal political contributions on the part of some corporations, many of which are international in their operations, cast a cloud of suspicion over every multi-national corporation. In the aftermath of this atmosphere, all of the old charges made against them were resurrected.

One commonly heard charge concerns the size and power of a multi-national corporation. It is said to possess such power that it can overwhelm all but the largest national states. One so-called fact cited to support this view is a comparison between the Gross National Product of a nation and the total sales of a major international corporation.

This comparison is essentially false. The gross sales of a corporation are not available to management for discretionary use. Moreover, there are numerous examples of nations that expropriated with impunity the assets of foreign companies whose annual sales exceeded the nation's GNPs.

THREE OTHER MYTHS

There are three other myths about American multi-national corporations that persist despite a preponderance of data to the contrary. They usually involve charges that multi-national corporations avoid taxes and export jobs and increase imports. In recent years, however, the Tariff Commission, Department of Commerce, and others have found that American companies have increased exports by $3 billion and in the process created between 500,000 and 600,000 domestic jobs between 1966 and 1971.

The positive contributions to this nation's economy made by Union Carbide and other multi-national corporations are the result of a "pull effect" exerted by the companies' investments in exports, largely in the form of allied, intermediate, and accessory products needed to complement the product lines of a foreign facility.

Union Carbide's experience supports these findings. The company has conducted and published the results of a study of the social and economic effect of its foreign investments over two decades. It shows that the company's foreign investments from 1951 to 1974 "pulled"

185

an additional $1 billion in exports from the United States which, in turn, produced an additional 2,500 export related jobs for workers in our domestic plants.

The social and economic benefits of multi-national corporations in host countries are equally important aspects of their operations. The companies' foreign investments have a "push effect" on the economies of these nations. The infusion of capital and technology, the introduction of training programs, the addition of jobs and payroll dollars for the payment of taxes both personal and corporate, and the creation of management opportunities for local nationals cannot but help host nations, particularly developing countries.

Despite these bilateral contributions made by American multi-nationals to international trade, a number of tax reform proposals are now before the Congress that would virtually eliminate American business ventures in foreign countries. The forced withdrawal of American multi-nationals from overseas markets would, in turn, have disastrous effects on our balance of payments and on domestic employment.

Two of the most counter-productive of these tax proposals involve the elimination or the reduction of foreign tax credits permitted foreign subsidiaries of American corporations and the taxation of income derived from those subsidiaries before its distribution to American shareholders.

In essence, these proposed tax reforms hark back to the Burke-Hartke bill of a few years ago. Then, as now, the old rhetoric is dusted off and pressed into the debate. Force the American multi-national to stay at home, so the argument goes, and more jobs will be created for U.S. workers and untold tax revenues will flow into federal coffers.

Nothing could be further from the truth.

Curbing foreign investment would not increase jobs at home for the simple reason that foreign markets cannot always be supplied competitively through exports. Nor do these foreign operations act as a drain on domestic employment. In fact, the opposite is true.

At Union Carbide, for example, one out of every

eight of its United States workers is employed in an export related job with more than half of the company's exports last year going to or through its foreign affiliates. Union Carbide's foreign operations, as with many other comparable American multi-nationals, act as a kind of magnet that attracts foreign sales of its American-made products.

More often than not, the choice for the American multi-national is between conducting foreign operations or not participating in them at all. The competitive realities of international trade dictate an American overseas presence to preserve market positions or to open new markets for its products. This cannot be accomplished from an executive suite in New York, Chicago, or San Francisco. It has to be directed on the spot.

The proposed tax reform changes now under consideration in Congress would, for the most part, place American multi-national corporations at such a disadvantage that a competitive vacuum would be created into which our foreign competitors would eagerly rush. In the case of the chemical industry this would be devastating. As it is now, seven of the world's top ten chemical companies are foreign owned. The adverse ramifications in terms of exports, balance of payments, and domestic employment would be far-reaching and virtually impossible to reverse. Elimination of the foreign tax credit would, in effect, impose double taxation, and this burden would be so great as to foreclose foreign investment for American business.

In the case of Union Carbide, this would mean an effective tax rate of about 70 percent for our foreign subsidiaries and affiliates. As George P. Shultz, then Secretary of the Treasury stated before the House Ways and Means Committee last year: "...the basic foreign tax credit must be understood not as a tax loophole...but rather as part of a system designed to allocate primary taxing jurisdiction to the government within whose borders the income is earned."

Foreign income tax rates are, in fact, generally as high as the U.S. rate. For example, tax rates in the 30 foreign nations where Union Carbide has manufacturing facilities are on the average as high as the United States statutory rate of 48 percent. Between 1966 and

187

1974, these taxes totaled $592 million, which represents a tax rate of 47 percent for this period — hardly an incentive to encourage foreign investment or tax avoidance.

Research conducted by the National Foreign Trade Council confirms that American direct investments in Canada, France, West Germany, Italy, Japan, the Netherlands and the United Kingdom bear approximately the same tax burden as does domestic investment. Even where the tax burden is lower — for example, Italy at 46.5 percent or Canada at 46.4 percent — the differences relative to the U.S. rate are too small to constitute a significant incentive for foreign investment.

The same basic flaws exist in the arguments to change the tax law so that the income of foreign subsidiaries is taxed *before* its remission to American shareholders. As the National Foreign Trade Council points out, there is no other country that taxes undistributed operating earnings of a foreign subsidiary. In fact, some countries never tax those earnings, whether or not they are distributed. The reason, of course, is because those earnings make a positive contribution to the maintenance and expansion of overseas trade, which, in turn, becomes an energizing factor for balance of payments and domestic employment. Again, let me stress that it is not the tax itself that is the bone of contention. In the case of the undistributed earnings, it is the timing. In the case of the foreign tax credit, it is simple equity with foreign competition.

RECOGNIZING ETHNOCENTRISM

Ethnocentrism is the tendency for people to feel their race, religion, culture, or nation is superior and to judge others by one's own frame of reference. **Frame of Reference** means the standards and values a person accepts because of his life experience and culture. A Marxist in Russia, for example, is likely to view things differently than a Christian in France.

Ethnocentrism has promoted much misunderstanding and conflict. It helps emphasize cultural differences and the notion that your nation's institutions are superior. Education, however, should stress the similarities of the human condition throughout the world and the basic equality and dignity of all men.

In order to avoid war and violence, people must realize how **ethnocentrism** and **frame of reference** limit their ability to be objective and understanding. Consider each of the following statements carefully. Mark (E) for any statement you think is ethnocentric. Mark (N) for any statement you think is not ethnocentric. Mark (U) if you are undecided about any statement.

E = ETHNOCENTRIC
N = NOT ETHNOCENTRIC
U = UNDECIDED

_____ 1. There is a massive loss of faith in the American business community by the American people.

_____ 2. Americans have no quarrel with profit-making, but they do resent unethical business practices at the public expense.

_____ 3. Federal laws should be passed making corporate bribes to foreign officials illegal.

_____ 4. Investments abroad by American corporations promote good will and economic growth.

_____ 5. Without U.S. technical help and business investments, many foreign countries would not be able to improve their economic life.

_____ 6. America is today the last great hope of the free world.

_____ 7. The multinational corporations exploit poor nations more than they help them.

_____ 8. The multinational corporation is one of the most creative economic institutions in the 20th century.

_____ 9. Mostly the term *free world* refers to those right wing military dictatorships that get their arms free from the U.S.

_____ 10. The United States is the strongest and greatest democracy in the history of the world.

_____ 11. The redistribution of economic and political power is the price of maintaining democracy in America.

_____ 12. We must permit large corporations to use bribery abroad or U.S. companies will not be able to compete successfully with foreign companies.

SELECTED PERIODICAL BIBLIOGRAPHY

Because most school libraries have a rather limited selection of books on economics, the editors have compiled a bibliography of helpful and recent periodical articles. Most school libraries have back issues of periodicals for at least a few years, and it is hoped that the following entries will be of some help to the student who wants to study American economics in more depth.

MORALITY AND VALUES

Walter F. Beran	*How to Be Ethical in an Unethical World*, **Vital Speeches**, July 15, 1976, p. 602.
Business Week	*After Watergate: Putting Business Ethics in Perspective*, September 15, 1973, p. 178.
	The Global Costs of Bribery, March 15, 1976, p. 22.
Milton Friedman	*The Uses of Corruption*, March 22, 1976, p. 73.
James Greene	*Ethics Not Customs: Corporate Misconduct Abroad*, **Vital Speeches**, October 15, 1975, p. 25.
Ivan Hill	*The Ethical Basis of Economic Freedom*, **Vital Speeches**, March 15, 1976, p. 345.
Carhl H. Madden	*Why We Must Have Industrial Growth*, **Nation's Business**, March 1976, p. 38.
Newsweek	*How Clean Is Business?* September 1, 1975, p. 50.
	Zapping Zero Growth, August 26, 1974, p. 60.
William Ophuls	*The Scarcity Society*, **Harpers**, April 1974, p. 47.
Marcus Raskin	*A Matter of Values*, **The Progressive**, October 1975, p. 19.
Howard Richards	*A Normative Economics*, **The Center Magazine**, May/June 1976, p. 36.

Ronald G. Ridker	*To Grow or Not to Grow: That's Not the Relevant Question*, **Science**, December 28, 1973, p. 1315.
Bayard Rustin	*No Growth Has to Mean Less Is Less*, **New York Times Magazine**, May 2, 1976, p. 13.
Mayo J. Thompson	*Morality and Free-Enterprise*, **Vital Speeches**, January 15, 1974, p. 202.
Time	*Profits: How Much Is Too Little?* August 16, 1976, p. 54.
Alexander Trowbridge	*Watergating on Main Street - Business*, **Saturday Review**, November 1, 1975, p. 18.
U.S. News & World Report	*Watergate May Turn Out to be a Catharsis to American Business*, August 26, 1974, p. 67.
Paul Verghese	*Develop — But Don't Grow!* **The Christian Century**, June 6, 1973, p. 653.

THE ROLE OF GOVERNMENT

David Bensman & Luther Carpenter	*Dead End of An Ideology*, **The Nation**, November 8, 1975, p. 456.
Jimmy Carter	*For America's Third Century Why Not Our Best*, **Vital Speeches**, December 15, 1975, p. 82.
Frank Donatelli	*Rebirth of Freedom*, **New Guard**, January/February 1976, p. 13.
John Kenneth Galbraith	*Capitalism's Failure*, **The New Republic**, August 16, & 23, 1975, p. 18.
Edward S. Herman & Richard B DuBoff	*The Urban Fiscal Crisis*, **Commonweal**, March 12, 1976, pp. 169.
Vernon E. Jordan	*The New Minimalism*, **Newsweek**, February 23, 1976, p. 9.
Richard L. Lesher	*Can Capitalsim Survive?* **Vital Speeches**, September 15, 1975, p. 731.
Frank R. Lyons	*Business and Government Controls*, **Vital Speeches**, December 15, 1975, p. 82.
Newsweek	*Big Government*, December 15, 1975, p. 34.

Robert Samuelson

Should We Be Bad Mouthing Government? **The New Republic**, May 15, 1976, p. 10.

Derek Shearer &
Lee Webb

How to Plan in a Mixed Economy, **The Nation**, October 11, 1975, p. 336.

U.S. News & World Report

Do States Have the Answers? August 18, 1975, p. 61. (an interview with three governors)

Getting Government Off People's Backs, October 6, 1975, p. 29.

BIG BUSINESS AND FREE ENTERPRISE

Robert Bosc

Questions for the American People, **America**, November 22, 1975, p. 355.

Allan C. Brownfeld

The Bicentennial and Private Property, **New Guard**, February 1976, p. 18.

Michael Harrington

The Big Lie About the Sixties, **The New Republic**, November 29, 1975, p. 15.

John R. Howard

A College President Addresses Corporate Leaders, **Vital Speeches**, November 11, 1975, p. 50.

Steven Philip Kramer and
Leo Friedman

Permanent Unemployment? **Commonweal**, August 1975, p. 360.

Sam Love

Let the Old Order Die, **The Progressive**, November 1975, p. 38.

Casper W. Weinberger

On Losing Our Freedom, **Newsweek**, August 18, 1975, p. 11.

TAX REFORM

Henry W. Block

The American Taxpayer: An Endangered Species? **Vital Speeches**, March 15, 1976, p. 332.

Milton Friedman

Tax Reform: An Impossible Dream, **Newsweek**, April 12, 1976, p. 93.

Vernon E. Jordan, Jr.

Black People On the Economic Front, **Vital Speeches**, September 15, 1975, p. 711.

Robert Lekachman

Redistributing Income, **The Nation**, May 11, 1974, p. 589.

The Nation

The Vanik Report, December 20, 1975, p. 644.

The New Republic	*Ho Hum Tax Reform*, December 13, 1975, p. 5.
Newsweek	*Biggest Bite*, August 4, 1975, p. 25.
The Progressive	*Tax Relief for the Rich*, September 1974, p. 8.
William K. Tabb	*Income Shares and Recovery*, **The Nation**, October 4, 1975, p. 299.
U.S. News & World Report	*Investigators Closing in on Offshore Tax Havens*, May 3, 1976, p. 61.
	Those Income Tax Rates Tell Only Half the Story, November 24, 1975, p. 90.

THE NATIONAL DEBT

John Kenneth Galbraith	*Why the Economy Is in a Mess*, **U.S. News & World Report**, November 3, 1975, p. 41.
Meg Greenfield	*Are We Too Generous?* **Newsweek**, September 15, 1975, p. 84.
Charles H. Smith, Jr.	*Can Freedom Survive in America?* **Vital Speeches**, March 1, 1975, p. 298.
Jude Wanniski	*The First $90 Billion*, **National Review**, March 19, 1976, p. 268.
James N. Wetzel	*The Federal Role In the Economy*, **Current History**, November 1975, p. 179.

SOCIAL SECURITY

John Conyers, Jr.	*Old, Sick, Scared — Social Security: The Bad Dream*, **The Nation**, May 8, 1976, p. 558.
William S.P. Cotter	*Social Security, the Frankenstein Monster*, **Vital Speeches**, November 1, 1975, p. 34.
Kiplinger Magazine	*Is Social Security Fair To Singles*, August 1974, p. 45.
Barbara Keoppel	*The Big Social Security Rip-off*, **The Progressive**, August 1975, p. 13.
Robert J. Meyers	*Social Security: Don't Push the Panic Button*, **America**, September 20, 1975, p. 140.

Newsweek	*Social Security: What Next?* January 19, 1976, p. 37.
The Progressive	*Social Security Nightmare*, April 1976, p. 8.
Time	*Social Security: No Bankruptcy — But a Need for Money*, February 16, 1976, p. 53.
U.S. News & World Report	*A Defense of Social Security*, February 24, 1975, p. 75.
	Fresh Scare Over Social Security, February 16, 1976, p. 68.
	Why So Many Feel They're Short-changed By Social Security, July 26, 1976, p. 37.

MULTINATIONAL CORPORATIONS

Gurney Breckenfeld	*Multinationals At Bay*, **Saturday Review**, January 24, 1976, p. 12.
Francis J. Dunleavy	*This Business of Conglomerates*, **Vital Speeches**, March 15, 1976, p. 338.
Bennett Harrison	*Inflation By Oligopoly*, **The Nation**, August 30, 1975, p. 145.
Vincent S.Kearney	*Come Home Multinationals!* **America**, May 8, 1976, p. 409.
Erik V. Keuhnelt-Leddihn	*From the Continent*, **National Review**, September 13, 1974, p. 1044.
The New Republic	*Ethics Gulf*, May 31, 1975, p. 3.
F. Perry Wilson	*The Highest Self Interest*, **Newsweek**, November 24, 1975, p. 23.
C. Wolcott Parker	*Bribery In Foreign Lands*, **Vital Speeches**, February 15, 1976, p. 281.
Michele Sindona	*From Multinationals to Cosmo-Corporations*, **Vital Speeches**, September 1, 1975, p. 689.
Tad Szulc	*U.S. and ITT In Chile*, **The New Republic**, June 30, 1973, p. 21.
George Wald	*There Isn't Much Time*, **The Progressive**, December 1975, p. 22.

meet
the editors

Gary E. McCuen received his A.B. degree in history from Ripon College. He also has an M.S.T. degree in history from Wisconsin State University in Eau Claire, Wisconsin. He has taught social studies at the high school level and is currently working on additional volumes for the Opposing Viewpoints Series.

DAVID L. BENDER is a history graduate from the University of Minnesota. He also has an M.A. in government from St. Mary's University in San Antonio, Texas. He has taught social problems at the high school level and is currently working on additional volumes for the Opposing Viewpoints Series.